The How-to Book of
Repairing, Rewiring, and Restoring
LAMPS and
LIGHTING FIXTURES

Also by Rachel Martens

MODERN PATCHWORK

The How-to Book of Repairing, Rewiring, and Restoring

LAMPS and LIGHTING FIXTURES

RACHEL MARTENS

All photographs by the author
Line illustrations by Thomas Gaskill

A DOLPHIN BOOK

Doubleday & Company, Inc., Garden City, New York   1979

Frontis: For chain lights using collectible glass shades see Chapter 13.

Library of Congress Cataloging in Publication Data

Martens, Rachel.
The how-to book of repairing, rewiring, and restoring
lamps and lighting fixtures.

1. Electric Lamps—Amateurs' manuals.   I. Title.
TK9921.M36   643′.3
ISBN: 0-385-14747-3
Library of Congress Catalog Card Number 78–66997

CONTENTS

ACKNOWLEDGMENTS

This book was made possible by the wholehearted support of Stan Angelo, Jr., president of Angelo Brothers, of Philadelphia. Thanks to him, I had access to the expertise of his company employees for any technical advice, and access to all the electrical supplies needed to complete each project. I also thank him for all the line drawings made available through his generosity. I owe gratitude to Jess Falini, creative director of Angelo Brothers, for his valuable advice and counsel.

I thank Nancy Hay for making her collection of antique oil lamps available to me and for permitting me to photograph the converted lamps in her restored eighteenth-century home. I also thank Albert Acker, of Wynnewood, Pennsylvania, and Tom Horner, of State College, Pennsylvania, for permitting me to photograph lamps and fixtures in their places of business; Gladys Cushman, of Portsmouth, Rhode Island, for permission to photograph the ceramic lamps in her shop; and Larry's, of Haddonfield, New Jersey, for co-operation in obtaining lampshades. I appreciate the suggestions on photography from John Gouker and the extra care Sigmund Jakaitis gave in processing my photographs for this book. I extend a special thanks to Kathryn Larson for her valuable editorial assistance.

The How-to Book of
Repairing, Rewiring, and Restoring
LAMPS and
LIGHTING FIXTURES

WHAT'S IN THIS BOOK FOR YOU?

This book begins with directions for taking a lamp apart, repairing and rewiring it, and putting it back together again— your basic Lesson One. If you are a confirmed do-it-yourselfer, chances are you've repaired many a plug or replaced many a socket; you may not need such elementary beginnings. But if your home care has stopped short of lamp repair, this is where you start. Then move on confidently to the rest of the book—your guide to finding some great old lamps and fixtures and figuring out how to make them beautiful and useful again.

There are step-by-step directions in this book for redoing more than thirty old lamps and fixtures; for installing dimmer switches, wall sconces, and chandeliers; for designing and making lamps from all kinds of collectibles or ceramics, and even directions for hanging plant lights to make your indoor garden grow.

Each type of project design includes a detailed list of the electrical supplies you need to complete the job—supplies readily available in your neighborhood from hardware, variety, and department stores, electrical-supply shops, and mail-order houses. When you know what to ask for (often, a prepackaged kit containing all the essential parts), getting started is easy. As you finish each project, you'll have learned techniques that will save you the cost of this book many times over.

Don't protest that you "can't do electrical work." You can do *this* electrical work; these are simple lamp repairs and installations. All you need is a little

know-how—and the basic safety rules— to give you confidence.

If you've ever waited days for an electrician to show up, or wondered why a five-minute job costs so much, you'll especially welcome the time- and money-saving ideas in this book. Actually, you'll be doing your electrician a favor if you learn how to make simple repairs yourself; professionals can't make a living on house calls for small jobs.

15

their value, you must first be able to recognize what you've found. So we have been conscientious about collecting examples of the various styles and types of lighting devices used in the United States since the 1830s (and before, if you count candlesticks).

A few of the lamps pictured are of museum quality; the rest are more typical of the kind and quality you'll find by prowling antique shops, flea markets, secondhand stores, and garage sales. Many of your finds—like ours—will be incomplete: pieces and parts in various stages of ruin, which you'll be able to buy at reasonable, even bargain, prices. Don't hesitate to snap them up. Any missing part you might need to restore a lamp to good working order is easily available from your electrical-supply or lamp-parts dealer.

If you spend weekends at flea markets, you anticipate the pleasure to be found in taking apart an encrusted piece of metal and seeing it emerge as a beautiful brass fixture. Or the creative fun in contriving lamps from all kinds of odd pieces never originally intended for lighting. The more you learn about lamp parts the more possibilities you'll see in junk, because you'll be able to visualize how to put it together or how to repair it. Look in Chapter 15 for some starter ideas.

If you are restoring an old house, you will be seriously concerned with authenticity. Are the fixtures you find on the property "of the period"? We've identified most of the old lamps and fixtures by date or era (e.g., "the gaslight era"), but these are examples, not the complete history. There are several excellent books on the history of lighting which you can consult if you need more help in identifying or verifying particular lamps, lamp parts, and fixtures (see end of chapter).

Our concern in this book is to show you how to restore and electrify old

In Chapter 10, you will see how easy it is to install a wall switch. But note that this book does not cover installing new outlets or making any changes in basic wiring. No behind-the-walls stuff. Such wiring must be done by experts and licensed electricians—for safety's sake and to abide by building codes.

RESTORATIONS AND CONVERSIONS

Much of this book concerns the rescue and rejuvenation of early electric lamps, or the conversion of old oil lamps and gas fixtures. Our intent is to give you more how-to than history; but if you respect old things and want to preserve

16

lamps and fixtures without destroying their value by drilling holes in them or taking away original parts. A good craftsman does not damage antiques. What is done to the lamp should be reversible; for example, you should be able to reconvert an electrified kerosene lamp to a kerosene-burning lamp.

Knowing what can be done and what shouldn't be done in lamp restoration is important even if you don't plan to "do it yourself." You will be a more discerning shopper if you learn what to look for in old lamps. You'll be in a better position to direct your repairman if you know what fittings are available and how they can be used to solve problems in various kinds of electrical conversions.

BEYOND CANDLEPOWER: Lighting Through the Eighteenth and Nineteenth Centuries

There is nothing in the dim, smoky light of oil-and-rag Betty lamps or rushlights that we yearn to recapture or convert to electricity. But we are still inspired by candles, a light source dating from Roman and medieval times. No matter what other kinds of lighting have come in, candles have never gone out.

We dine romantically by candlelight in the twentieth century, and we use the candlestick form for many of our lamp and fixture designs. It's completely functional as an electric lamp; it's also a pleasing and appropriate accessory in any room, any decorating period. It looks right because it's always been around—through every design period, in every country, for every kind of home from castle to cottage.

Chinese vases imported via England, classic urns, and hand-blown bottles are other house furnishings from colonial days ideally shaped to serve as lamp bases. In fact, many new lamps are cop-

ies of such designs; like candlesticks, they belong in almost any-style room.

Old vases, candlesticks, and bottles have antique value and should never be electrified by mutilation. To wire them without drilling holes, use adapter kits as shown in Chapter 3 (bottle lamps), and Chapter 6 (vases). For five ways to turn a cherished candlestick into a lamp, turn to Chapter 4.

OIL LAMPS

Whale oil and other burning-fluid lamps, popular from 1830 to 1850, were early efforts to step up light intensity; but when a Canadian geologist named Abraham Gesner patented a process to produce kerosene, in 1852, it proved to be the answer—fuel for safe, dependable

17

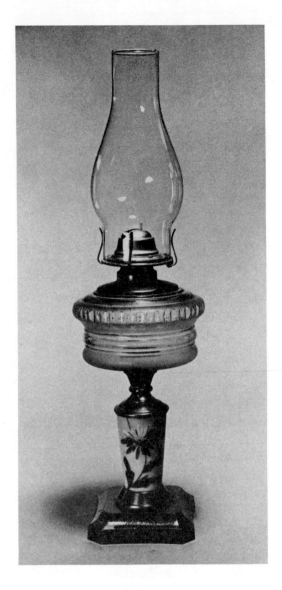

the peg light; it literally substituted for a candle. It had a small, onion-shaped bowl with a glass peg at the bottom that fit into any candlestick. You simply moved the lamp from candlestick to candlestick. The hand lamp came along shortly: a font with low base and a handle, like a cup handle, so you could carry it from room to room.

Bracket lamps became favorites for bedrooms and kitchens. The frame, attached to the wall, was hinged so the lamp could swing out into the room (see page 75). Some bracket lamps had shiny reflectors of mercury glass or tin.

The word "overlay" describes lamps that became popular between 1850 and 1860; they had cased-glass fonts—two layers of glass with the top layer cut away in spots to show the color below. This lamp usually had a marble base and a brass stem.

Assembled lamps were exactly that—assembled from parts made from various materials and designed to be fitted together: a stone or black-iron base, brass fittings, and a glass font (see page 56). The 1880s lamp often had a frosted, pressed-glass font with a hand-painted design on a china or glass stem. Figure-stem lamps were also popular; cast in metal, sometimes gilded, the figure held up the oil font.

The student lamp, an extremely popular novelty lamp between 1875 and 1900, was engineered so that it wouldn't cast a shadow on the working surface of a desk or writing table. It had a detachable font that fed through tubes to a burner on the opposite side. See how to electrify it on page 83.

In 1888, a lamp with a central-draft burner and a round wick was introduced by Rochester. Rayo, Miller, Alladin, and others adopted the design. It's the easiest of all oil lamps to electrify. Thanks to the opening through the center of the font,

light. Kerosene lamps sold well into the 1920s—even thirty years longer in rural areas (some manufacturers are still making them). Though kerosene as a lighting fluid didn't change during this time, the lamp designs proliferated and evolved considerably through the years. Now being sought by collectors and nostalgia buffs, these lamps are still in plentiful supply and are affordable.

The earliest of the kerosene lamps was

there's no need to drill holes for lamp pipe, switches, or cord. See how to wire on page 80.

Banquet lamps of the same era were tall enough to light the entire room when placed in the center of a table. The tall brass stems (sometimes figurines) were topped with ornate brass or glass fonts 15″ to 18″ above the table surface.

The late-Victorian era was ornamented with parlor lamps that typify that golden, sometimes gaudy, age. Even though electricity was gaining ground at about the same time, there was a final big surge in fancy oil lamps of all kinds— some more for decoration than for seeing by. Some with flat wick and a vase-type font that held the oil. Some with central draft and a brass oil font hidden inside the vase. Originally selling for as little as 95 cents, the parlor lamps now command big money—especially those that haven't been mutilated when converted to electricity. Even more rare is one with its original, painted shade. If you are lucky enough to locate an unelectrified parlor lamp, there are directions for wiring it starting on page 89.

GASLIGHT

Though kerosene provided the light in a majority of U.S. homes during the last half of the nineteenth century, gas came into use at the same time—at first only in the more affluent sections of cities. Brass or bronze chandeliers were hung from living-room ceilings, and many were trimmed with crystal prisms and chains. They looked elegant!

Newel-post lights for the spacious hallways of townhouses were quite elaborate. And there were countless designs, simple and ornate, for bracket lights and wall sconces. Many of these fixtures have such graceful shapes, they're being sought today by collectors and designers involved in restoring old houses.

Considering the variety of design in gaslight fixtures, they are relatively easy to electrify. The sconce we worked on (see page 126) was chosen to illustrate the type of fixture you're most likely to find and shows how to wire it. The sconce you find may not be of exactly the same construction, but the techniques will apply. You'll find examples of gas table lamps on page 115.

Though chimneys on kerosene lamps

19

were always clear glass (and some used reflectors) to throw as much light as possible into the room, the more brilliant flames of gaslight needed shielding to prevent uncomfortable glare. Designers outdid themselves fashioning all kinds of domes, globes, and shades in frosted, pressed, opal, and colored glass. Few of the chandelier shades survive as complete sets, but we show you how to salvage the singles by hanging them as chain lights (see page 156).

ELECTRIC LIGHTS

At the turn of the century, electric lighting developed to the point of practical use, and in the thirty-year span from 1890 to 1920, consumers had a wide choice of lamps in all three types of illumination: kerosene, gas, and electric. There were even fixtures that combined two light sources, such as kerosene and electricity, or gas and electricity—a practical idea in those early days when electricity was not so dependable. The kerosene or gas flame was an up light, shielded with a glass shade; the electric bulb was directed down and had a matching glass shade. Coming in around 1920, the earliest all-electric chandeliers had candle-type sockets with, at first, ordinary bare bulbs. When shades were added, they were of metal or silk.

In rural areas, electricity was a luxury until the end of World War II, when the government program of rural electrification (REA), begun in the thirties, raised power lines along every highway in America. Before that, homes outside city limits used kerosene as a light source, or even gasoline! "With this light," the ads read, "it is possible for the farmer in the most humble circumstances to have light equal to millionaires." Coleman was an important producer of gas lamps and lanterns; you'll find them today—electrified —in many antique shops.

The greatest innovator in lamp design during the Art Nouveau era was Louis C. Tiffany, a member of the famous jewelry family. Even in 1900, his lamps were expensive; now, the second time around, they command the highest prices. His leaded-glass shades are copied today by lamp manufacturers; even those copied from other designers of this era are sometimes labeled Tiffany-type.

In direct contrast to the sinuous lines of Art Nouveau, the next design move-

20

ment was Art Deco, characterized by straight, heavy lines, geometric designs, chrome, and glass. For lamps of both design eras, see Chapter 9.

HOW THIS BOOK WILL HELP YOU

Everyone has a lamp that goes on the blink at one time or another. Usually all it needs is a new socket or a new wire. Instead of taking it someplace to be fixed, you can repair it yourself. From simple repairs to restoring old lamps is an easy progression. With the step-by-step photos in Chapter 1, you can even make a brand-new lamp from a column of chrome if that's what you want.

In Chapter 2 you learn how to shop for a shade for the lamp you've made— or for a replacement shade. Lamps can be repaired, but cloth shades wear out and glass shades break. We describe shade materials, sizes, and types, explaining what to look for, how to get the right fit, what goes with what in glass shades.

As you get acquainted with the various old or antique lamps and fixtures shown in this book, you'll recognize the influence of past periods on today's new lamp designs. Candlesticks, vases, urn shapes—they're as popular as they ever were for lamp bases. And many shiny new fixtures are evocative of the gaslight and oil-lamp eras. But the good reproductions are expensive. In order to know that you're getting your money's worth, it's helpful to study the originals.

Many collectors and decorators are opting for the original antiques when they restore or redecorate period homes. For about one third more, you can get an original fixture or lamp, one that will increase in value—providing you don't mutilate it when you wire it. If you learn nothing else from this book, you'll learn how to electrify lamps without altering them or destroying their value as antiques!

Anyone who accepts the challenge of restoring an old house will investigate what kind of lighting the house should have. That means learning something about the house's past, along with enough lighting history to match that period. One of the common errors is to put beveled-glass carriage lanterns at the front door in the belief that they look

21

House, Watkins Glen, New York. From primitive home lighting through electricity; illustrations include reproductions of old ads and catalog pages.

2. *A Heritage of Light,* by Loris S. Russell, University of Toronto Press, Toronto, Ontario, Canada. Many choice lamps and fixtures of museum quality illustrate the lighting periods.

3. *Flickering Flames: A History of Domestic Lighting Through the Ages,* by Leroy Thwing. Exhaustive coverage of early lighting from prehistoric beginnings to kerosene lamps.

4. *Oil Lamps: The Kerosene Era in North America,* by Catherine M. V. Thura, published by Wallace-Homestead Book Co., Des Moines, Iowa. Comprehensive coverage of the kerosene years with more than one thousand beautifully photographed lamps.

Old lamp catalogs are invaluable sources, if you can find them (even these are being snatched up by collectors). If you can't find them, at least consult reprints of old Sears catalogs; the most recent one, called The Best of Sears Collectibles, 1905–1910, has a seventeen-page section on lamps.

In this book, we have tried to give you enough of an overview of lamp history to whet your appetite to learn more if you want to . . . to become a discerning collector. But in lamps and light fixtures, collecting isn't the end of it. Inevitably, your finds will need some work, and if you learn how to do the restoration and repair work yourself, you compound your pleasure.

With this knowledge, you can do whatever interests you most. Research your finds so you'll know what part is needed to make the restoration authentic. Or wing it: devise your own solutions from your own sense of what will work and what will look right. Parts and sup-

"colonial." The carriage lantern didn't make the scene until about 1865; most are later models manufactured in the eighties and nineties. The true Paul Revere lantern is not round, punched tin, as many ads lead you to believe. Tin wall sconces do not belong in a Georgian manor house; a crystal chandelier is not for hanging in an old farmhouse.

How do you learn what goes where? By delving into lamp history. And four good books to help in this search for authenticity are:

1. *New Light on Old Lamps,* by Dr. Larry Freeman, published by Century

plies are easily available at hardware, variety, and department stores, or from electrical-supply dealers—everything you need to pursue this creative and rewarding hobby. Who knows? You may develop it into a source of extra income or a full-fledged business.

This lamp is a flea-market find. Though shadeless and wobbly, it was a good buy for six dollars. The lamp base, imported from the Mideast, is of pewter-washed copper; the design is copied from the metal bottle (also pictured) used in Mediterranean countries. The base measures 14″ to the bottom of the harp. The shade, 12″ deep, 14″ in diameter, is of linen laminated to vinyl.

CHAPTER 1

HOW TO REWIRE A LAMP

This chapter will tell you—if you don't already know—how to rewire a lamp. If you've done a lamp or two, you know there's nothing mysterious about it and it's not difficult. But don't tell your friends how easy it is. Let them think you're some kind of electrical wizard.

If you have never replaced a socket or a cord, you can teach yourself in one easy lesson. Maybe you have a flickering lamp—one you've been meaning to get fixed. Buy a socket, and a new cord if you need it, and use the lamp to learn by. The pictures that follow show you how to take it apart and put it together again, step by step.

Once you've repaired a lamp (have threaded cord through lamp pipe and twisted wires onto socket terminals), you have the basic know-how to salvage all kinds of attic relics and flea-market finds —to say nothing of designing your own lamp bases from bottles, wood turnings, candlesticks, and other *objets d'art*.

Don't let anyone scare you about rewiring a lamp. All you have to remember, to avoid a shock, is to unplug the lamp from the wall outlet before you begin. If you somehow manage to get it wired wrong (most unlikely), when you plug it in again the lamp simply won't light. It won't spit or sputter or burn the house down. What is dangerous is to keep on using a lamp when you know the lamp cord is frayed (exposing the wire) or there's a short circuit in the socket. Such a lamp should be repaired—and you can do it!

Almost every standard table lamp will be wired as shown in the step-by-step pictures that follow. Later chapters will cover some variations, but most projects will refer back to Steps 9 through 14 for wiring a socket.

Now inspect the lamp you want to repair and collect the supplies and tools you'll need to finish the job. Here is a checklist of what you'll need.

SUPPLIES YOU WILL NEED

- socket
- harp and finial
- brass neck, threaded to screw onto the lamp pipe
- knurled brass locknut
- nipple, about ½″ long (needed only if the original lamp didn't have a neck)
- lamp cord with molded-on plug
- lamp pipe, if you need to replace the old one
- lockwasher
- washer
- hex nut

These are the parts you will need for most lamp wiring or rewiring jobs, though you may not need to buy all these parts new. You must be the judge of what can be salvaged from your old lamps. When in doubt, be safe and replace with new parts—especially the socket and the wire.

You'll be able to find the first six items in kits—conveniently prepackaged for you. (Look for them in mail-order, department, and hardware stores, in vari-

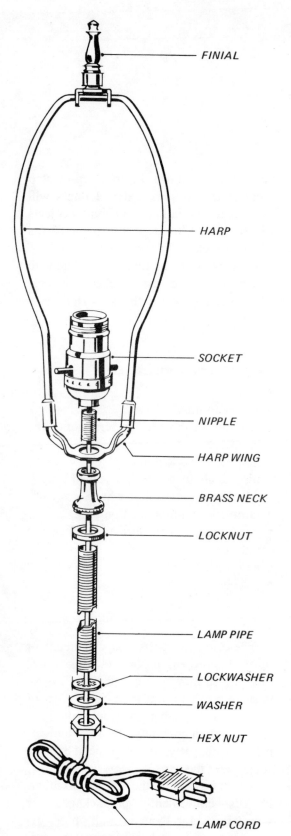

FINIAL

HARP

SOCKET

NIPPLE

HARP WING

BRASS NECK

LOCKNUT

LAMP PIPE

LOCKWASHER

WASHER

HEX NUT

LAMP CORD

ety, hobby, and electrical-supply shops.) Or you can buy any of the pieces you need separately.

TOOLS YOU WILL NEED

- screwdriver
- pliers (sometimes two will come in handy)
- wire stripper if you have one, a sharp knife if you don't
- hacksaw, for cutting lamp pipe

These common, everyday tools are the only ones you need for most of the wiring projects in this book.

TRADE TERMS

When you rewire a lamp, you need cord and other supplies in standard lamp sizes. It's usually sufficient to tell your dealer you want the items to repair a lamp. But just so you know, the trade specifications are as follows: lamp cord, No. 18; lamp pipe and nipples, ⅛-IP; nuts threaded to fit the ⅛-IP pipe and nipples; washers with holes just large enough to slip over the pipe and nipples. See Glossary for a more complete definition of terms.

DISASSEMBLING THE LAMP

Step 1

Unplug the lamp from the wall outlet. Remove shade and bulb. If the lamp has a two-piece harp, remove top part from the harp wings so you'll have more room to work. To do this, lift up the two metal sleeves that lock the harp pieces together, squeeze harp, lift out.

Step 2

Take the socket apart. A socket comes in four pieces: outer shell, usually of metal; cardboard insulator sleeve; socket with terminal screws; socket cap.

To take the socket apart, press down with your thumb on the outer shell where it's marked PRESS and pull apart. If it is stubborn or corroded, pry open with a screwdriver. Then remove metal shell and cardboard insulator to expose wires.

Step 3

Loosen the two screws in the socket to release wire ends of lamp cord. Pull cord out through bottom of lamp. Unscrew socket cap from center rod. If it doesn't come off easily, steady the center rod by gripping hex nut at base of lamp with pliers and twisting the cap forcefully.

Step 4

Remove harp wings, locknut, neck, and washers from the top of the lamp. Then the rod is free, so you can pull it out.

ASSEMBLING THE LAMP

Step 5

Skip this step if you don't need to replace the pipe in your lamp. But if you do, use a hacksaw to cut a piece of threaded lamp pipe the length you need; use the old piece of pipe as a guide. (If you clamp the rod into a vise for sawing, use several layers of cloth between vise and rod to protect the threading.)

Before you cut, thread two nuts onto the pipe—one on each side of the cut mark. After you make the cut, remove the nuts; as they're unscrewed, they'll clean off any burrs. Use a metal file to remove any sharp edges on pipe ends.

Step 6

Insert pipe into lamp base. Secure it at the bottom with a washer and hex nut. You can now thread lamp cord through the side hole of the wood base and up the center rod (or you can wait to thread the cord after the socket cap is in place).

Step 7

If your lamp is hollow (like this one), you'll need a weight inside—on top of the solid wood base. (For a lamp with a hollow metal base, add the weight inside the base.) Not all lamps need weights, but ballast is desirable if the lamp is lightweight and easily tipped over, especially after the shade is added.

Step 8

Screw a brass locknut firmly (by hand) onto the top of the lamp pipe; then screw on the brass neck.

NOTE: If the lamp you're redoing didn't have a neck, you can add one; a neck usually improves the appearance of the lamp. Screw neck onto lamp pipe; then screw a ½″ nipple into the neck; attach socket to nipple.

Step 9

Slide harp wings onto the lamp pipe (or nipple) before you screw the cap of your new socket to the rod. Don't forget these harp wings—you'll be furious if you discover them on the table after you've wired the socket.

Pull up the lamp cord so you have a comfortable 6″ or 8″ to work with. Slit the insulation between the two wires of the cord for about 2″—start slit with a sharp knife and pull wires apart. Tie an ordinary knot in the cord just below the split; leave it loose. (Purpose of this knot is to keep tension off the wire ends when there's a tug on lamp cord.)

Step 10

Remove about ½″ of insulation from the end of each wire—with a wire stripper if you have one, with a sharp knife if you don't.

Step 11

Twist all the exposed fine copper wires clockwise between your fingers—tightly so they'll stay together.

29

Step 12

Bend twisted wire ends into U shapes and wrap each around one of the two screws of the socket—clockwise. It doesn't matter which wire goes to which screw.

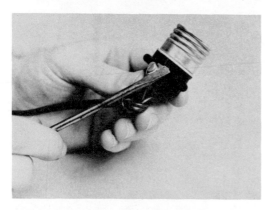

Use the screwdriver blade to coax the wire ends under the screw. Tighten screw —tight as you can get it—so ends won't pull out. Check to see that no straggling loose wires are left exposed.

Step 13

Now tighten the knot in lamp cord— push it as close to bottom of socket as possible. Seat the socket in the cap; pull extra lamp cord down (from the base).

30

Step 14

Slip the cardboard insulator over the socket. Then seat the outer metal shell firmly into the socket cap; you'll hear it click into place.

Step 15

For a professional touch, add felt to the base of the lamp. It will protect your furniture and also hide the hardware in the lamp base.

Step 16

You are now ready to add the top of the harp and finial and go shade shopping. That's all there is to it!

Heavy brass candlesticks (English) are wired into a distinctive pair of lamps and mounted on wooden lamp bases shaped to fit the candlestick base. They're made taller with candle spacers (see how-to steps, this chapter)—in good proportion to the heavy Victorian desk. Shades are handmade, from antique embroidered linen.

CHAPTER 2

HOW TO CHOOSE A LAMPSHADE

Buying a shade is like buying a hat: the only way you can come up with a winner is to try it on for size.

Knowing the dimensions of the old shade should be enough, but it doesn't guarantee a good fit. Not all manufacturers use the same frame system, so some shades "sit higher" than others. A slight variation in shape or a different material may change the total look. In such cases, your eye is more trustworthy than a tape measure. When you shop, always, always take the lamp base with you.

Here are other guidelines to keep in mind:

- The depth of the shade should be about 2″ less than the height of the base. If the shade is deeper than that, the lamp tends to look top-heavy. The shade can be shallower; in fact, if the lamp base is very slender, a shallow shade will seem to have a more pleasing proportion.
- At eye level, the bottom of the shade should be even with the bottom of the harp (or socket). If the socket shows, either the shade is too skimpy or the harp is too deep.
- Don't worry if the shade you like doesn't fit the harp you have. Buy a new harp—it will add less than a dollar to the cost of the shade. If the harp on your lamp is new, chances are you can make an even swap for the right size—at least in better lampshade shops. Since harps come in two parts, it's easy to make the switch. You won't have to rewire the lamp.
- Choose a shade that's appropriate for the base. Usually a plain shade is the best companion for a decorated base; a textured burlap or linen shade pairs well with crockery, while an exquisite porcelain base demands a fine, hand-sewn shade.
- The shade should help the lamp perform its job. For general or mood lighting in a living room, you can use a dark, opaque shade if that suits your room. But, on a dressing table you need translucent white shades to spread light evenly for makeup.

When you bring a new shade home, remove any cellophane wrapped around it immediately. The heat from a lighted lamp dries cellophane; as it loses moisture, it tightens. And it's strong enough to compress the lamp frame and warp it —permanently.

SHAPES AND SIZES

There are three basic shade styles or shapes: drum, empire, and bell-shaped. In most shade stores, you'll also find some specialty shapes mixed in with the standard.

Whatever the shape, the lamp size is described by the diameter of the bottom of the shade. A 12″ shade is one that measures 12″ across the bottom. Hexagonal shades are measured (at the bottom) from point to point, oval shades by the longer diameter. The depth of the shade is the top-to-bottom (vertical) measure. When three dimensions, such as 8″ by 9″ by 6″, are used to describe a

Drum shade

Empire shade

shade, it should be read as 8″ across the top, 9″ across the bottom, and 6″ deep.

Drum shades are drum-shaped. They appear to be straight up and down, but the diameter of the top is actually 1″ smaller than the bottom. Depending on the depth of the shade, you'll call it a shallow drum, regular drum, or deep drum.

Empire shades have sides that slope; there is a difference of 2″ or more between top and bottom diameters. When the sides are severely slanted (such as 4″ by 10″ by 5″), the shade is called "cone" in some shops, "umbrella" in others.

Bell shades have curved sides shaped by wire ribs running up and down between top and bottom rings. These ribs are bent inward to form the bell shape. All bell shades are fabric; paper and other stiff materials cannot follow the curve of the ribs.

Specialty shades come in a generous variety of shapes, though selection will vary from store to store. You may find square, oval, hexagonal, and cut-corner square shades. Some may have a scalloped edge. In addition to regular bells, there are square and cut-corner square bells, hexagonal, octagonal, and scalloped bells. More unusual shapes include pagodas, Tiffany domes, and shades with S-curved spokes.

Vanity and candle shades may have a corner all to themselves in any well-stocked lampshade department, because they are small and their use is so specialized. Shapes are the basic drum, empire, and bell shapes. Vanity shades, for bedroom, boudoir, or dressing-table lamps, are 6″ to 12″ in size. Candle shades are smaller, 3″ to 5″, and are used mainly on fixtures—chandeliers and wall sconces—but also on candelabras.

TOP-OF-THE-SHADE FITTINGS

At the top of the shade there has to be a device for attaching the lamp shade to

Bell shade

the lamp base or lamp bulb. The lamp design dictates whether you need a shade with a washer, a chimney ring, a uno ring, or a clip-on fastener.

The **washer-type shade** is the most common. It's used on lamps with harps —and most table lamps have harps. The washer, in the center of a three-pronged spider fastened to the top rim of the shade, fits over the finial stud on the harp. Usually the spider is bent slightly, to bring the washer below the top of the shade.

At the beginning of this chapter, we suggested that it's easy to change harps if the harp you have doesn't fit the shade you've found. To determine the size harp needed, measure from the washer straight down to the bottom of the shade. Even if you have a large, deep shade, you will almost never need more than a 12″ harp, because the deeper the shade the deeper the bend in the spider. For example, a standard shade 15″ deep very likely will have the washer sunk 3″ so you can use a 12″ harp.

Spiders on large-sized shades are crimped to sit on reflector bowls; many floor lamps and some large table lamps have these. The crimp keeps the shade from shifting. (See drum-shade illustration.)

The **chimney shade** has a recessed inner ring fastened to the top of the shade. The ring, about 2½″ in diameter, is designed to slip over a glass lamp chimney. This kind of shade is especially useful for oil- and gas-lamp conversions. Not only does it give you opportunity to add color and pattern, it also covers the glare of the bulb. Bottom of shade may be from 5½″ to 9″ in diameter.

The **uno shade** is used only on lamps with sockets that hang down: some bridge lamps, some Art Deco lamps. It has a 1½″ threaded ring in the center top of

Shade with washer-type fitting

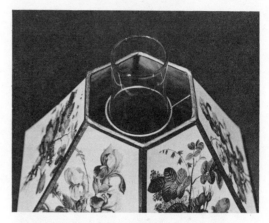

Chimney shade with a recessed inner ring

Uno shade

Clip-on shade; comes with either round clamps (top) or oval clamps (below)

Shade riser

Socket extension

the shade which screws onto the shell of the socket.

The **clip-on shade** has two wire circles fastened across the top of the shade which clamp onto the light bulb. This shade is most suitable for small lamps; you'll seldom see it used on a lamp more than 9″ tall. But it is often the choice for boudoir or vanity lamps or pin-ups; also for lamps placed on furniture above eye level—on a high chest of drawers, for instance.

Most shades for chandeliers, wall sconces, and candelabras are clip-ons. In tiny sizes (from 2″ to 4½″), they come with round clamps for standard bulbs, or oval clamps for flame bulbs.

HARDWARE TO MAKE SHADES FIT

Shade risers: If you need to raise a shade only an inch or so, you don't need a new harp. Get a shade riser—available in lengths from ½″ to 2″—and screw it onto the finial stud. Then attach shade and finial.

The same hardware can be used as a finial riser. When the shade is in place, screw one (or more) risers onto the finial stud until high enough to bring the finial above the shade.

Socket extensions: When you find a clip-on shade you like, but it sits about an inch too low on the base, you can use a socket extension to lift it up. Simply screw the socket riser into the existing socket.

This extension also comes in handy when you change bulb sizes. Bulbs of different wattages or bulbs ·by different manufacturers may vary as much as an inch in height. A socket extension will raise the bulb—and the shade.

Adapters: If you find exactly the shade you want but with the wrong fittings, don't pass it by. There are several small devices that clip or snap into shade fittings. One style (a) will change a washer shade into a clip-on; another (b) will

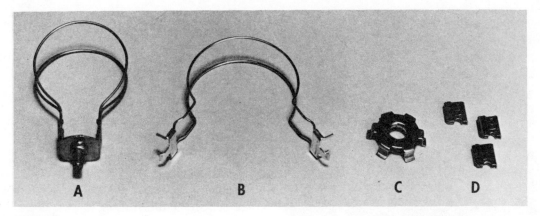

Adapters

change either a washer or uno shade into a clip-on. Another adapter (c) changes a uno shade to a washer shade. And there are clips (d) which make it possible to use any uno or washer shade on a lamp with a reflector bowl: clips clamp onto the spider and keep shade from shifting.

MATERIALS FOR LAMPSHADES

Lampshades are described as "soft" or "hard" depending on the material used to make them. The soft shade—always of fabric—is stretched over a framework of wire ribs between top and bottom rings. But for a hard shade, there is no need for framework other than top and bottom rings. The shade material—vinyl or paper—is stiff enough to separate and support the rings.

The most practical and durable material for **hard shades** is vinyl. The heavy, white, translucent vinyl used today is a great improvement over paper: it doesn't yellow or deteriorate with age. Nor is it easily creased or damaged. ·

Vinyl may be used alone; more often, some kind of fabric will be laminated to it: linen, grass cloth, shantung, cotton prints, burlap. Pleating and fluting add even more variety to vinyl shade designs. (See drum-shade illustration.) Best of all, you can clean the vinyl shade or vinyl lining with a damp cloth.

Some of the paper shades still availa-

Opaque paper shade

Knife-pleated fabric shade

the frame will be completely wrapped with fabric strips. Another sign of quality is a "no-shadow" frame, with ribs bent in such a way that they don't show at all when the lamp is lighted.

The best fabric shades are hand-sewn. If pleated, each knife pleat is stitched down by hand. Around top and bottom, there will be a French binding—a strip of fabric, folded like bias tape to hide the raw edges, and stitched down by hand. (See bell-shade illustration.)

A well-made shade will also have a rustproof finish on the frame; it's designed to tolerate scrubbing with soap and water. But before you dunk a fabric shade, inspect it carefully. Cheap shades are put together with glue and staples; if washed, the glue dissolves and both frame and staples rust.

NOTE: On a hand-sewn shade, fabric is stitched to the frame while damp—it tightens as it dries. In damp weather it may become slack. The remedy is simple: just turn on the light, and the heat from the bulb will tighten it again.

ble are treated to look like parchment. This material is used most often for shades with scenics or for hexagon-shaped shades with panels of birds or flowers. Instructions with these shades suggest cleaning them with furniture polish. (See chimney-shade illustration.)

Another type of paper shade is opaque, sometimes with a high-gloss finish on the outside, white on inside, sometimes with a brushed-brass effect on the outside. Opaque shades for tole lamps are metal.

Soft shades are commonly called "silk shades," though now only the most expensive of them are made of pure silk. The materials used most often are nylon, Celanese, and rayon. To hide the ribs in the framework, soft shades need a lining —some even have an interlining. And in the best-quality, top-of-the-line shades,

GLASS SHADES

The earliest shades were made of glass —fireproof protection against open flames or tipped-over oil lamps. As you would expect, few of the original very early shades survive; every year, more of them make the casualty list through breakage. So there's always been a thriving business in glass replacement shades.

The places to look for glass shades are in electrical shops, in some hardware and mail-order stores, and in lampshade shops. There's such a variety of glass shades being manufactured, no store can stock everything that's made. So if you can't find what you want, ask to see a catalog. Most dealers will special-order what you need.

For oil lamps, there are two basic styles of replacement shades: the globe (a ball) and the hemispherical shape (half a ball).

For gaslight fixtures, there are a variety of designs in bowl-shaped shades; and for electric fixtures, untold shapes and sizes of shades to cover individual bulbs—many duplicating some of the highly collectible (and costly) art glass shades.

Another type of glass shades in high favor are those labeled "Tiffany-type"—most often used for table lamps and swag or chain lights.

Tiffany-type glass shade

OPAL GLASS AND OTHER TYPES OF GLASS

"Genuine opal" is the favored material for glass shades. The term describes a milky-white glass that glows when light shines through it; no finish applied to plain glass can duplicate the richness of this light. Another attribute, important to china painters who duplicate antique designs "to match the base" of late-Victorian lamps, is that the genuine opal shades can take kiln firing (up to 900° F).

"Satin opal" refers to a finish for glass that may have been either fired on or sprayed on by the manufacturer. If the finish is fired on, the shade can be painted and subsequently kiln-fired, but a sprayed-on finish cannot be fired.

"Cased glass" is another important type of replacement glass shade. It refers to a shade with an outer layer of colored glass (most often green) bonded to a layer of white opal glass. These shades are becoming more and more difficult to find, and they command premium prices. So if you come across one that's priced right, buy it.

You'll have no difficulty finding a replacement shade made to look like cased glass. The color is painted and then fired onto an opal glass base. When the light is turned on, you can easily tell the difference: the painted finish lacks the vibrant glow of genuine cased glass. But the price is right.

You will also find glass shades on the market that duplicate old-fashioned pressed-glass patterns, including hobnail and quilted glass, as well as etched and cut designs.

SHAPES AND SIZES OF GLASS SHADES

The most common shapes in replacement shades are student, tam o' shanter, dome, globe, ball, and gaslight—plus a variety of shapes for electrical fixtures.

Student shades, sometimes called Rayo shades, are hemispherical. The most common sizes are 6", 7", and 10" in diameter. They're made in opal glass, cased glass, and pressed glass (melon and swirl patterns are especially popular); and in plain colors as well as hand-painted designs. The flange around the top may be plain, flared, or fluted.

These shades are used on student lamps and brass lamps (such as Rayo, Rochester, Miller, Hubbard & Bradley, etc.); on

Student shade

Tam o' shanter shade

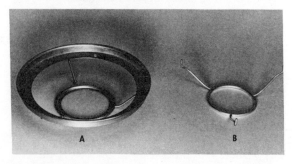

Ring holder (a) and tripod (b) for dome or student shade

glass oil lamps, and on some of the hand-painted late-Victorian lamps.

Tam o' shanter is a variation on the shape of the student shade—not so deep, more like the beret from which it gets its name. It's a well-proportioned shade for lamps that have a squatty font (oil reservoir); also for tall, columnar lamps that can take a shallow shade.

Dome shades have the same hemispherical shape as student shades; they're simply larger—14″ in diameter. They fit large banquet lamps and hanging fixtures, and come in opal glass, cased glass, transparent amber, and ruby glass, and in etched or painted designs.

Dome shades and student shades (including tam o' shanter) rest most securely on ring holders (a), which can be ornate or plain, with or without prisms. Originally, before the ring holders came along, a dome shade was held up on a wired tripod (b), sometimes called a spider. If you yearn for authenticity, you can still buy it. But a ring holder helps cut down on breakage.

Globe shades are spherical, from 3″ to 14″ in diameter, graduating in 1″ increments. They're open at top and bottom to accommodate the lamp chimney; around the bottom opening there's a flange which rests on a ring called a fitter. The most common fitter size is 4″, in a range from 1⅞″ to 5″.

Opal glass is by far the most popular material for globe shades—especially now that so-called Gone With the Wind lamps are coming down from the attics. Since few of the original globes still survive, china painters are busy duplicating the old designs—on opal glass, since it can be painted and fired.

Frosted glass with or without cut designs is also a popular material for globe shades, especially for glass oil lamps. Globes also come in hobnail, quilted, and painted designs, and in clear amber or ruby glass.

Ball shades look like globe shades, except there's no opening for a chimney. The ball shade is designed to hang down —in swag lights, hanging lamps, and ceiling fixtures; also under Tiffany-type hanging shades. (See page 157.) The ball shade has a flange opening for a fitter (most take a 4″ fitter), and on the opposite side the glass may have a ⅝″ opening to take a finial-like ornament. The most common sizes available are 6½″, 8″, 9″, and 10″ in diameter.

Plain ball globes are made of opal glass, sprayed satin glass, and in a milky-white plastic. They also come in colored glass—embossed, swirled optic, or crackled; and in pressed- and cut-glass patterns.

Gaslight shades available today are bowl-shaped, for the most part, copies of those made originally for gas chandeliers and wall sconces. Because light from a gas flame was so much brighter than kerosene light, it was necessary to design shades, to cut glare. That's why most gaslight shades are made of frosted glass. Highly desirable are hand-blown shades with hand-shaped fluted edges, in colored or candy-striped glass.

If you are electrifying a gaslight fixture, your largest choice will be among shades that duplicate pressed-glass designs. Most gaslight shades have 4″ fitters.

Glass fixture shades defy general description; they come in far too many shapes, designs, and sizes to tabulate: in modern and traditional designs; perfectly plain, or in a variety of pressed, etched, or cut designs; frosted or clear; in hurricanes—your choice of straight, flared top, or tapered body.

Fitter sizes run the gamut: about 8 sizes, ranging from 1⅝″ to 4¾″ (the most common is 2¼″). So be sure to measure the fitter on your chandelier—accurately—before you shop for replacement glass shades.

41

A globe shade of frosted glass with cut design

Gaslight shade of frosted glass

A flared-top hurricane-style glass shade

This glass bottle has graduated from filtered-water container to lamp base. The socket fits into the neck of the bottle—no drilling necessary. Its rich brown color blends well with the octagonal floral shade. Finished lamp is 23″ tall.

CHAPTER 3

HOW TO WIRE A BOTTLE LAMP

In most lamp designs, the cord runs through the center of the lamp base and out the bottom. But it is possible to make a lamp from a bottle without running a pipe through it or drilling a hole in the bottom.

Why would you want to avoid drilling? Several reasons. If your bottle is valuable—a hand-blown antique or a lovely old decanter, for example—you don't want to risk it. Drilling might shatter the glass, or at the very least ruin its value as an antique. If your proposed lamp base is some inexpensive but interestingly shaped jug or amusing wine bottle, it's hardly worth the trouble or expense of having it drilled.

To wire a bottle without drilling, you need a socket with a side outlet and an adapter to hold the socket snugly in the neck of the bottle. The cord comes out through the side of the socket, above the bottle. If you choose a cord color that blends with the color of the bottle, you'll hardly notice it—especially if you place the lamp on a table or chest with the cord falling off at the back. Or you can tape the cord at the back of the bottle, near the bottom, to keep it out of sight.

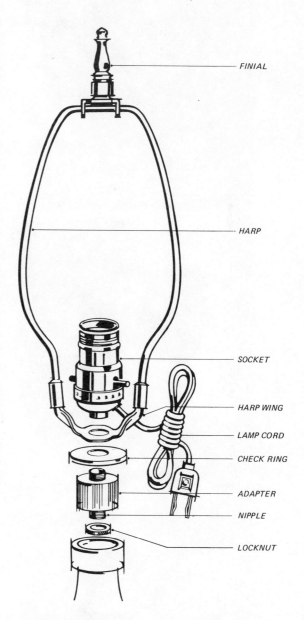

FINIAL

HARP

SOCKET

HARP WING

LAMP CORD

CHECK RING

ADAPTER

NIPPLE

LOCKNUT

SUPPLIES YOU WILL NEED

- socket with side outlet
- harp and finial
- knurled brass locknut
- rubber adapter—in a size to fit bottle opening (available from 5⁄8″ to 1¼″, can be shaved to fit in-between sizes)
- brass check ring—choose size to fit over top of bottle
- threaded nipple, 1½″ long
- lamp cord with molded plug

For your convenience, you'll find kits with all the above parts in hardware, department, mail-order, and variety stores; also, electrical supply and hobby shops.

STEPS FOR WIRING BOTTLE LAMP

Step 1

Choose an adapter to fit the bottle opening. You want a snug fit, but don't use force when working with delicate glass. Antique glass, especially, becomes brittle with age and may shatter. If the fit is too tight, shave rubber with sharp knife or razor blade.

Step 2

Insert a threaded nipple into the rubber adapter. Leave about ¼″ exposed on top side—for the socket and harp wing.

Screw locknut to bottom side of nipple, all the way up until it touches the adapter. This keeps nipple from lifting out when you screw on the socket. Tightening causes the rubber to expand somewhat, so you may need to do some additional shaving; a metal file does a good job of minor whittling.

Step 3

Push rubber adapter with nipple into bottle neck until it is flush with top of bottle. Then set brass check ring in place over the top to cover the rubber.

44

Step 4

Place harp wing over check ring; screw socket cap onto threaded nipple and thread lamp cord through the side hole. (For a large bottle, add another locknut between check ring and harp; it gives a more secure fit to carry the heavier shade.)

Step 5

Wire socket as illustrated in Steps 9 to 14, Chapter 1. Then add harp, shade, and finial.

If the neck of your bottle is long, you'll have a more secure fit if you use a longer nipple and thread two adapters onto it.

Wire an ordinary wine bottle—it will throw a cheerful light onto your game-room or patio refreshment table. For a bottle that's 9″ or less in height, you can eliminate the harp and use a clip-on shade.

Brown-glass beehive-bottle lamp, 21″ tall, is a cheerful addition to any kitchen table. Its graceful shape is emphasized by the empire shade of pleated gingham vinyl.

This crockery jug lamp adds a cheerful accent light to the brick-topped plant window. Shade of grass cloth over pleated vinyl blends with the base both in texture and color.

The completed candlestick lamp is 20″ tall—ideal for bedside or dressing table. If you use the lamp on a tall piece of furniture, consider eliminating the harp and using a clip-on shade.

CHAPTER 4

FROM CANDLESTICK TO LAMP

All through the ages, in every country, designers have given us beautiful candlesticks. In early days, candles provided the principal source of light and candlesticks were a necessity. Today, candlelight is a sometimes event and the candlestick has become a "decorative accessory" —something to look at and admire.

But you can change that status. Thanks to the electrical supplies available to you, you can convert these unused candlesticks into lamps you use every day. Whether you have candleholders of glass, brass, silver, iron, ceramic, or wood, you can turn them into lamps appropriate to every room in the house. Useful as reading lights on desks and end tables; as accent lights on a hallway table, mantel, or buffet; perfect for bedside or dressing tables.

To make this conversion, you won't have to drill a hole in the candlestick or in any way destroy its value as an antique. Moreover, you can continue to use it with candles any time you wish—the wired socket lifts out as easily as a burned-out candle. After a candlelit evening, you can put the light socket back again, add the shade, and plug it in.

In this chapter, we show five different ways to convert your favorite candlestick into a distinctive lamp.

WIRING A CANDLESTICK WITH A BOTTLE KIT

The easiest way to convert a candlestick into a lamp is to wire it like the bottle lamp described in Chapter 3, plus a one-inch neck—the neck lifts the socket above the candlestick top. Without the neck, the shade would cover the top of the stick or the socket would show— neither of which would look right.

SUPPLIES YOU WILL NEED
- Bottle kit (or equivalent supplies) as shown in Chapter 3
- ½" nipple
- 1" brass neck
- another round locknut

How to wire:

Start with an adapter that fits snugly into the candlestick socket and add the nipple, locknut, and check ring; screw on the neck; add ½" nipple and another locknut; slip on harp wings; then wire on a socket with a side hole as illustrated in Chapter 1, Steps 9 through 14.

It's the same 10″ candlestick—wired two ways. The lamp on the left has a shade 9″ deep plus a 1″ neck to make a lamp 20″ tall. The lamp on the right has a shade 11″ deep plus a spacer to make the lamp 25″ tall. Best part about wiring candlesticks this way is that you can use them for candlelight at the dinner table merely by lifting out the adapter and works; convert them back into lamps as easily after the party is over.

ADDING A SPACER TO A CANDLESTICK LAMP

To make a candlestick lamp taller, you can insert a simulated candle—or spacer—between adapter and socket. For the spacer in the lamp shown, we used a 4″ length of white plastic tubing 1¼″ in diameter, slipped over a 4″ lamp pipe.

To make this conversion without drilling a hole in the candlestick, use a brass coupling with a side hole (instead of a socket with a side hole) and a regular socket. The cord runs from socket through lamp pipe and out, sideways, through the coupling and spacer.

SUPPLIES YOU WILL NEED

- adapter to fit candlestick socket
- lamp pipe, 4″ long
- brass coupling with side hole
- nipple, 1″ long
- 2 brass locknuts
- 2 check rings, 1¼″ diameter
- plastic tubing, 1¼″ diameter, 4″ long
- socket
- harp and finial
- lamp cord with molded plug

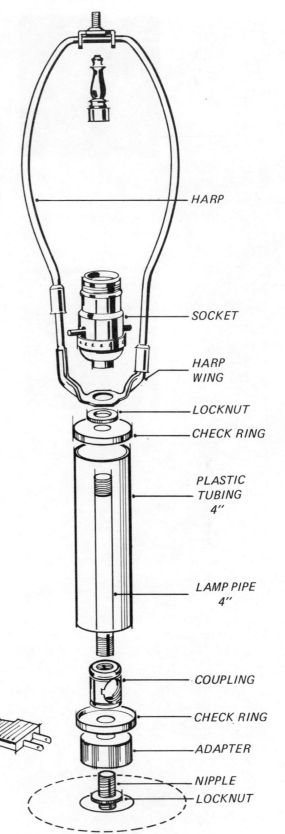

HARP

SOCKET

HARP WING

LOCKNUT

CHECK RING

PLASTIC TUBING 4″

LAMP PIPE 4″

COUPLING

CHECK RING

ADAPTER

NIPPLE

LOCKNUT

LAMP CORD

51

Step 1

Select an adapter that fits the socket of your candlestick. Shape it to fit snugly into the socket: whittle it down with a knife or use a metal file for minor shaping. If your candlestick takes a standard tapered candle, you'll need to start with an adapter about ⅞" in diameter.

Slip a 1" nipple into the adapter (which is ¾" deep), leaving ³⁄₁₆" exposed on top and enough on the bottom to secure it with a locknut.

Step 2

Slip a 1¼" check ring over the nipple, with the cupped side facing up (the plastic spacer will fit into it). Screw the coupling with a side opening onto the nipple. (You will now see why the nipple should extend only about ³⁄₁₆" above the adapter: more depth would close the side hole through which the lamp cord will be threaded.)

Step 3

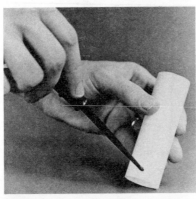

Bore a hole into the plastic tubing about ¼" from the base; make the hole just large enough for the lamp cord to pass through. You can melt a hole through the plastic with an ice pick or awl heated on the burner of your kitchen range.

Step 4

Feed the lamp cord through the hole in the plastic tubing (from outside in), through the side hole of the coupling, up the section of lamp pipe. (It's easier to thread the cord through before screwing the pipe into the coupling.)

Step 5

Screw the lamp pipe into the coupling. Gradually lower the plastic tubing over the pipe; pull out excess cord as you go.

Step 6

Add a 1¼″ check ring to the top of the tubing, with cupped side facing down. Secure it with a round brass locknut.

Add harp wing; screw on socket cap. Wire socket as described in Chapter 1, Steps 9 to 14.

Step 7

Add harp, shade, and finial.

Some candlesticks may have an opening through the center, top to bottom. Someone may have drilled a hole through. The stick could have been manufactured as a lamp base. Or the candle pusher may have been removed (that's the mechanism in the center of the candlestick used to eject candle stubs). To wire these candlesticks, follow the steps used for the lamp in Chapter 1.

Right:
Candlestick with an opening through the center, fastened to a base that has a side hole for the lamp cord

Far right:
Wrong way: Do not drill a hole through the base of the candlestick—it destroys its antique value. Furthermore, a hole drilled into metal needs a grommet to protect the lamp cord from friction with sharp edges.

This ornate candlestick is made of silver-plated brass. It's 14″ high; 20″ with candle socket. If you prefer to shield the flame bulb, use a clip-on shade. You could also wire this candlestick with a standard adjustable socket that takes ·a standard-size bulb— following the same steps as for the candelabra socket.

WIRING A CANDLESTICK WITH A CANDELABRA SOCKET

If you need an accent light in a hall-way, on a sideboard, or outdoors on the patio, you may prefer to fit a candlestick with an electrified candle—an unshaded, flame-shaped bulb in a candelabra socket. For a realistic effect, cover the socket with a plastic candle cover molded to look like a candle dripping wax. Flame-shaped bulbs come clear or frosted, in a range of sizes, shapes, and wattages.

SUPPLIES YOU WILL NEED

- rubber adapter to fit candlestick opening
- brass coupling with side hole
- nipple, 1″ long
- nipple, ½″ long
- 2 brass locknuts
- 2 lockwashers
- brass check ring, 1¼″ diameter
- waxlike plastic candle cover, 5½″ long
- adjustable candelabra-base socket (from 3¼″ to 4¾″)
- lamp cord with molded plug
- cord switch
- candelabra flame bulb

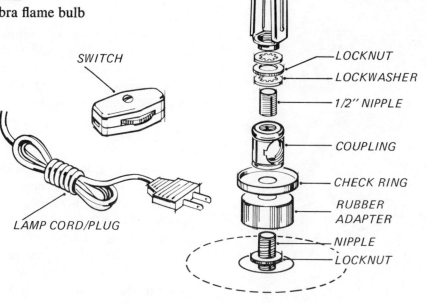

CANDLE COVER

INSULATOR W/CANDELABRA BASE

ADJUSTABLE CANDELABRA BASE

LOCKNUT

LOCKWASHER

1/2″ NIPPLE

COUPLING

CHECK RING

RUBBER ADAPTER

NIPPLE

LOCKNUT

SWITCH

LAMP CORD/PLUG

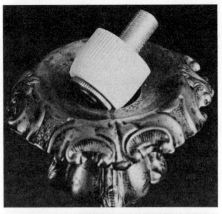

Step 1

Select an adapter that fits the socket of your candlestick. It's important to get a snug fit, especially if the candlestick hole is shallow. Use a metal file to taper the adapter for an exact fit. Insert a 1″ nipple into the adapter, leaving ³⁄₁₆″ exposed at the top and enough at the bottom to secure it with a locknut.

Step 2

Add a 1⅛″ check ring over the nipple, with cupped side facing up—to hold the candle cover in place. Screw a coupling with a side hole to the nipple.

Step 3

Screw the short, ½″ nipple into the top of the coupling. Add a lockwasher, locknut, and another lockwasher on top of it. Then screw the adjustable candelabra socket onto the nipple.

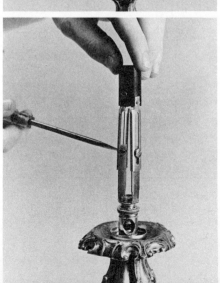

Step 4

Loosen the side screws on the adjustable candelabra socket, adjust to desired height, and tighten screws. For the full height of 4¾″, you'll need a candle cover that is ¾″ taller—5½″ in all. (The coupling adds to the height of the socket.) If the plastic cover is too long, you can always cut some off the bottom.

Step 5

With a hot ice pick or awl, melt a hole in the plastic candle cover, ¼″ from the bottom, just large enough for a lamp cord.

Thread lamp cord through the candle cover (from outside in), through side hole of coupling, up the center of the adjustable socket. Tie a knot in the cord close to the base of the socket. Then wire socket as in Chapter 1, Steps 9 to 14.

Step 6

Place cardboard insulator over wired socket—the notch rests on the Phillips Screw head (the one with the cross), completely covering both wired screws in the socket.

Step 7

Slide the candle cover over the socket, gently pulling on surplus cord as you lower cover.

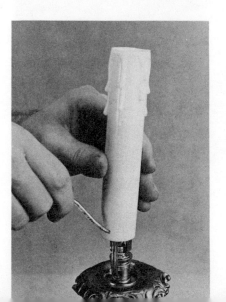

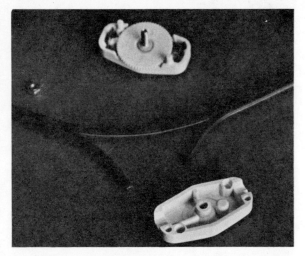

Remove the center screw to open the switch; lay aside the half that has the turn knob. Cut one wire in the lamp cord and pull each end apart for about ¼".

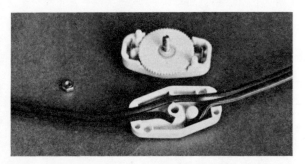

Lay the uncut wire of the lamp cord in the long channel of the switch; feed the cut ends into compartmented side, as shown.

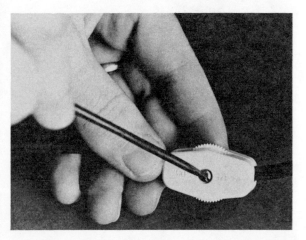

Press the top half of the switch onto the wired half. Screw back together. You're finished!

Step 8

Since there is no switch on the candelabra socket, you'll need to add one in the cord. Installing the switch is easy as a, b, c.

Add a candelabra bulb (its base is smaller than that of a standard bulb), plug into the wall socket, turn on the cord switch, and enjoy.

WIRING A CANDLESTICK FOR A HURRICANE SHADE

SUPPLIES YOU WILL NEED

- 2 rubber adapters to fit candlestick opening
- brass coupling with side hole
- brass inlet bushing to fit coupling side hole
- nipple, 1¼″ long
- nipple, ½″ long
- round brass locknut
- check ring, 1¼″ diameter
- brass glass holder, 1⅝″ fitter
- adjustable candelabra socket (from 3¼″ to 4¾″)
- waxlike candle cover, 5¾″ long
- *bobêche* 4″ diameter, with hooks for
- 6 crystal teardrop prisms, 2″
- clear, silver lamp cord with molded plug
- switch for cord
- flame bulb
- hurricane shade, 8″ tall, 1⅝″ fitter

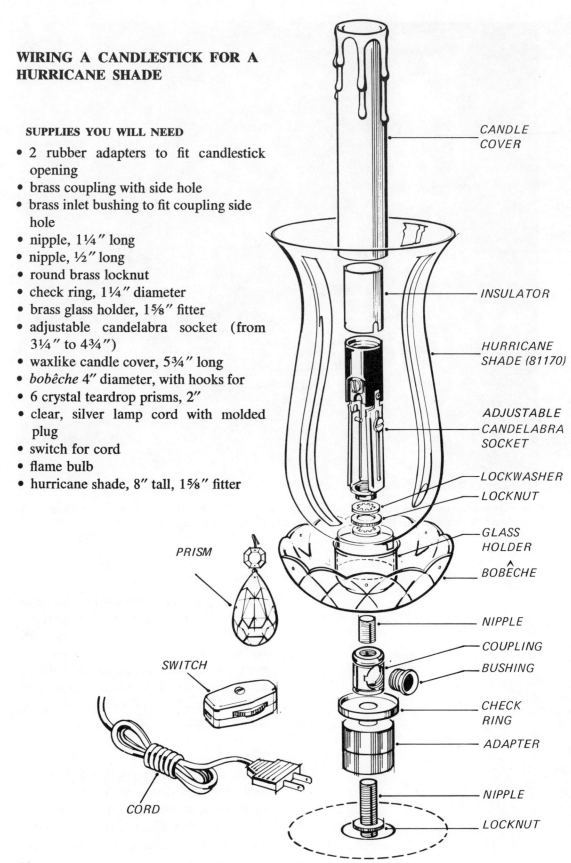

CANDLE COVER

INSULATOR

HURRICANE SHADE (81170)

ADJUSTABLE CANDELABRA SOCKET

LOCKWASHER

LOCKNUT

GLASS HOLDER

BOBÊCHE

NIPPLE

COUPLING

BUSHING

CHECK RING

ADAPTER

NIPPLE

LOCKNUT

PRISM

SWITCH

CORD

Clear-glass candlestick with a bubble stem is 10″ tall, 20″ when wired as a hurricane lamp. It throws a sparkling accent light in any room of the house.

Adding a hurricane shade will make an electrified candle more important-looking—a decorative accent light especially suitable for mantel or buffet. For even more pizzazz, place a *bobêche* under the shade holder and hang it with prisms—especially effective with glass candleholders.

Step 1

Select rubber adapters that fit the candlestick socket. Shape to fit—with sharp knife or metal file. The candle socket in this 9″ glass candlestick is deep enough for two adapters; that extra support is desirable for supporting the weight of a hurricane shade. Also, you need part of one adapter to extend above the top of the stick so the *bobêche* can be fitted over it—keeps *bobêche* from shifting back and forth.

Insert a nipple that extends the depth of both adapters, plus ¼″ extension on top. Secure with a locknut screwed to bottom of nipple. Then insert into candlestick socket.

We photographed it to show both rubber adapters; it will look better if you cover the rubber with silver foil or paint it silver to blend with the glass.

Step 2

Set *bobêche* over rubber adapter. Slip check ring over nipple—with cupped side down to hide adapter.

Screw brass coupling—the one with the side opening—onto the nipple. (Since this coupling will be exposed, be sure to polish it up first.) Then screw a brass bushing into the side hole of the coupling; it covers the rough edges, gives a more professional, finished look.

Screw the ½″ nipple into the top of the coupling.

Step 3

Slip the brass shade holder into the nipple. Add a lockwasher, locknut, lockwasher; then screw on the adjustable candelabra socket as for previous candlestick. Thread lamp cord through the side hole of coupling and up center of socket. (The clear, silver cord blends with crystal *bobêche* and candlestick.)

Adjust height of candelabra socket, wire as in Chapter 1, Steps 9 through 14. Slip on the cardboard insulator and wax-like candle cover.

Add the switch at a convenient spot in the lamp cord as for previous candlestick. Screw in candelabra-size bulb. Set hurricane shade into holder. Hang crystal prisms on *bobêche* hooks.

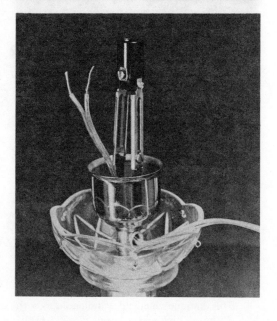

WIRING A CANDLESTICK WITH A DOUBLE FIXTURE SOCKET

If you want to make a tall lamp from a low candlestick, you can do it—with a 12″ length of plastic tubing to use as a spacer. This gives rise to another problem in design which is easily resolved with standard equipment. A tall, pole-like lamp base should have a relatively shallow shade. But a shallow shade won't hide the usual upright harp, light bulb, and socket. What you need is a double fixture socket to hold light bulbs horizontally. This will provide good light with no glare from bulbs hanging too low.

This antique Sheffield candleholder with an attached candle snuffer measures 5″ by 7″ by 4″ high. As a lamp, it's 20″ tall. It's wired with silver lamp cord to blend with the holder. The hand-sewn oval shade is 10″ by 14″ by 7″.

- rubber adapter to fit candlestick opening
- nipple, 1″ long
- nipple, ⅜″ long
- 2 round locknuts
- 2 hex nuts
- 2 check rings, 1¼″ diameter
- plastic double fixture socket
- white plastic tubing, 1¼″ diameter, 12″ long (length depends on height of candlestick—for tall stick, use shorter piece of tubing)
- threaded lamp pipe, 11¾″ long (¼″ shorter than tubing)
- steel hickey, threaded both top and bottom to take lamp pipe
- 2 plastic wire connectors
- reducer nozzle (from nipple size to finial stud)
- lamp cord with molded plug
- lamp-cord switch

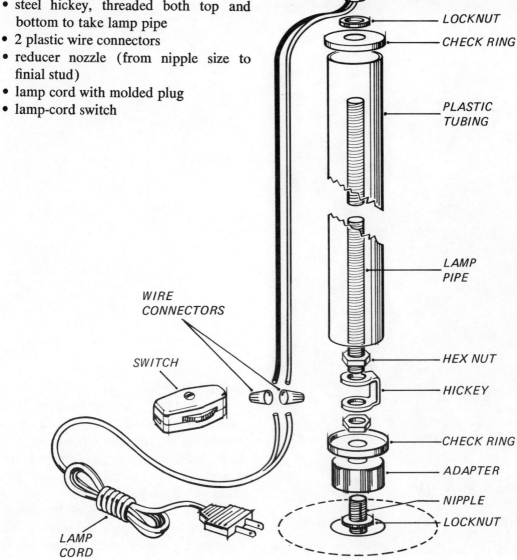

REDUCER NOZZLE

NIPPLE

DOUBLE-FIXTURE SOCKET

LOCKNUT

CHECK RING

PLASTIC TUBING

LAMP PIPE

WIRE CONNECTORS

SWITCH

HEX NUT

HICKEY

CHECK RING

ADAPTER

NIPPLE

LOCKNUT

LAMP CORD

Step 1

As for other candlesticks in this chapter, start by fitting a rubber adapter into the candle socket. Then insert a nipple into the adapter that's long enough so you can secure it at the base with a locknut and have ¼″ exposed at the top. It's important to get a snug fit, since this adapter will have to hold a 12″ upright supporting the weight of a shade. Use two adapters if the socket is deep enough.

Slip a 1¼″ check ring over the nipple with cupped side up (to hold the 1¼″ tubing); tighten with a hex nut.

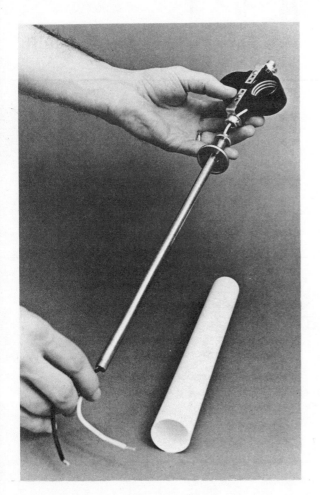

Step 2

Cut an 11¾″ piece of threaded lamp pipe with a hacksaw—¼″ shorter than plastic tubing. Slip the other check ring onto the top of the pipe, cupped side down. Screw a locknut onto the pipe about ¼″ down from top.

Thread the two wires of the double socket through the pipe and screw socket onto the top until it meets the locknut.

Step 3

Tighten the screw on the neck of the fixture socket. Screw a hex nut onto bottom of lamp pipe, to about ¼″ from the end. Then screw the small hickey onto the pipe until it meets the hex nut. The socket wires will exit sideways—from the center of the hickey.

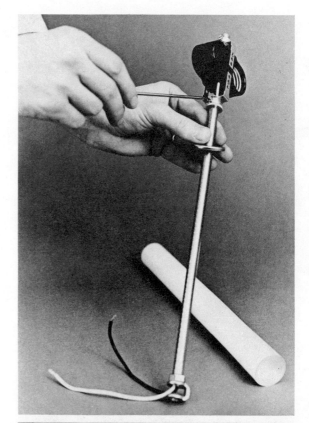

Step 4

With a hot ice pick or awl, melt a hole in the plastic tubing, about ¼″ from the base, just large enough for lamp cord to pass through. Then cover the assembled socket and lamp rod with the tubing.

Cut off surplus socket wires to a length of about 2″ or 3″ below the end of lamp pipe.

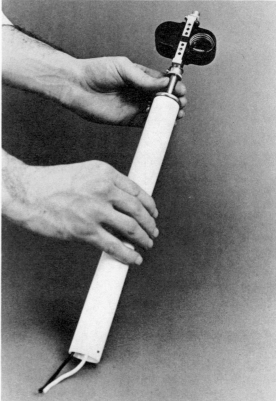

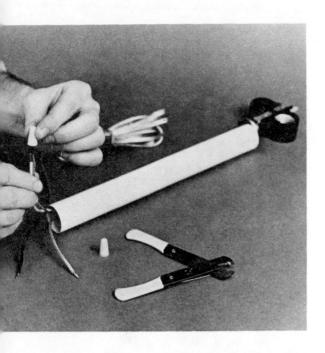

Step 5

Thread lamp cord through hole in the plastic tubing, from outside in. Split the two wires apart—for same distance as exposed socket wires (2″ or 3″). Strip the ends of all four wires—for about ¼″.

Now you are ready to splice the socket wires to lamp cord wires. To do this:

- Hold the end of one lamp cord wire even with the end of one socket wire (doesn't matter which one) and
- slip a small plastic wire nut over the wire ends and twist clockwise—just as you screw the cap onto a tube of toothpaste.
- Repeat for other two wire ends. Unbelievably easy! And so much simpler than fussing with electrician's tape or a soldering iron.

Step 6

Push the spliced wire ends up into the plastic tubing, one on each side of the lamp pipe to keep it centered.

66

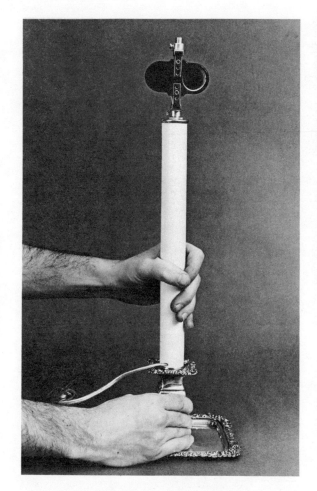

Step 7

Now screw the hickey end of the lamp pipe onto the exposed nipple in the candlestick socket—making sure that the plastic tubing fits into the top and bottom check rings. Be sure the hex nuts fit up snugly against the hickey; they add support and rigidity to the upright.

Step 8

Since the double socket is designed for ceiling fixtures, it doesn't have a finial stud. You can add one by screwing a ⅜″ nipple into the top of the socket and adding a reducer nozzle with a finial stud.

These electrified whale-oil lamps are of pressed glass, the cable-and-ring design. Fitted with clip-on shades covered in off-white linen, they provide good light with appropriate period design for the Sheraton chest and Queen Anne mirror.

CHAPTER 5

HOW TO ELECTRIFY OIL LAMPS

WHALE-OIL LAMPS

Whale-oil and other burning-fluid lamps are in great demand, because, like candlesticks, they're appropriate to the period of early-nineteenth-century homes. And they're easily converted to electric lamps. They are the first upright lamps (about 10″ to 11″ tall from top to table), the first lamps with vertical wicks, the first with enclosed containers to hold the oil. The elongated font, tapering from top to base, is the identifying shape; another identifying feature (if it hasn't been lost) is the metal tube or tubes for the wick. Whale-oil lamps almost never carried chimneys or globes.

A graceful choice for many rooms, electrified whale-oil lamps are true to the period of the early 1800s. Typical designs (left to right above): 1. Sandwich lamp, lyre pattern. 2. Pear-shaped glass lamp with bull's eye and fleur-de-lis design. 3. Vaseline Sandwich-glass lamp topped with fabric-covered shade. 4. Composite lamp with a blue overlay-glass font, brass stem, square marble base. 5. Pressed-glass lamp with diamond-point design. 6. Cut-glass lamp by Sandwich.

The whale-oil flame was not very bright; it smoked and had a bad smell. So there were endless experiments trying to find a better burning fluid. Such mixtures as whale oil with camphene and alcohol with turpentine were tried—often with disastrous results; the light improved, but some of the mixtures were highly explosive. It was necessary to design new burners. In one improvement, the metal wick that extended below the collar of the whale-oil lamp was moved up—away from the explosive fluids. And Ben Franklin gets the credit for designing a burner with two tubes instead of one. He had observed that two flames side by side give off more light than two separate lamps.

Burning-fluid lamps reached their zenith between 1824 and 1850. As the fuel got more explosive, the glass fonts became heavier. The earliest glass whale-oil lamps had thin blown-glass bowls, often pear-shaped, which were attached to pressed-glass stems. In later oil-lamp designs, both fonts and stems were pressed

Kerosene lamps put together with parts—fonts, stems, and bases—are called "assembled" or "composite" lamps. By shopping antique shows, you realize how many variations there are: seldom will you find two lamps exactly alike. The sampling pictured above suggests the possibilities: 1. Blue hobnail glass font, brass stem, enameled iron base (fabric-covered opaque shade). 2. Swag design on glass font, brass fittings, marble base. 3. Cross-cut design on glass font, opaque glass stem with brass fittings, slate base (opaque shade with metallic brass finish). 4. Shield design on glass font pressed in three-part mold, brass stem, marble base. 5. Plain glass font, two-piece brass stem, marble base (stick shade). 6. Small lamp in foreground is molded in one piece—not a composite.

glass—many in colored glass. The heavier glass necessary for burning-fluid lamps also offered opportunity for the interesting pressed patterns. And then came the composite lamps: a glass font attached to a brass stem screwed to a square marble base.

Lamps made by Sandwich Glass Works and New England Glass Company are the most sought-after by collectors.

To electrify whale-oil lamps: Use a screw neck adapter, socket with a side hole, and follow step-by-step directions given on page 74 for the kerosene lamp wired for a harp.

GLASS KEROSENE LAMPS

Kerosene or coal oil replaced all other burning fluids around 1860. It was safer to use, threw a better light, and was cheap enough so everyone could afford to burn it.

At first, kerosene was used in burning-fluid lamps with the round, solid-core wicks. But experiments to improve the quality of the light continued, and finally the flat-wick burner evolved. It had a sprocket to raise and lower the wick so you could adjust the flame and wick as it burned. It also had a device to hold a clear-glass chimney—a new invention which protected the flame from drafts and cut down the smoking. It was now possible to change the design of the font, too, from the elongated shape to a spherical or onion shape.

Kerosene-burning lamps caught on fast, and almost every glass manufacturer started making lamp bases. To this day, the collector can find an infinite variety of the shapes, sizes, and styles that were

1. Urn-shaped font of etched glass with red flashed-glass design, brass stem, marble base. 2. Pressed-glass font with etched design on panels, blue overlay, and brass stem; milky glass base. 3. Frosted font with cut thistle design in clear oval areas; font is fitted both top and bottom with brass; opaque blue glass base extends halfway up the stem. 4. Flashed-glass font on brass stem, marble base. 5. Frosted font with clear stripe (pumpkin pattern), blue glass base.

Glass oil lamp, before and after electrification. This antique lamp, molded in one piece, has a drip-catching channel around the top. It's 8″ tall and takes a No. 1 wired burner (shown in "before" picture). For a more graceful effect, we replace the plain, stubby-looking chimney with a flared-top chimney, beaded around the top.

offered, from the inexpensive plain molded glass to the more expensive cased-glass and cut-glass designs.

Also on the market: modern reproductions of old lamps, a revival that coincided with the back-to-nature movement along with organic foods and used-denim pants.

Wiring a kerosene lamp

Changing a lamp from oil to electricity is the easiest conversion of all.

You can buy the prewired converter, complete with cord and plug. It simply replaces the burner with a socket burner; there are prongs attached to hold the chimney.

All it takes is a twist of the wrist; screw out the old burner, screw in the new, wired burner. Add the bulb, fit the chimney back into place, and you have an electrified lamp.

Most electrified lamps need some kind of protection from glare. For shade ideas, see opposite page.

It's the same electrified oil lamp shown on previous page—with a chimney shade added. Inexpensive shade of dotted swiss over vinyl, ball-fringe trim, is especially appropriate for bedrooms. It measures 12″ in diameter, 5″ across top, 6″ deep.

ADAPTER AND CHIMNEY SIZES

Oil-lamp burners come in various sizes, determined by the size of the neck opening. So be sure to look for the electrified adapter that matches the size of your oil lamp. Here's a ready reference table to guide you when you shop:

burner size	opening size	chimney-fitter size (bottom diameter)
No. 00	⅝″	1⅛″
No. 0	⅞″	2⅛″
No. 1	⅞″	2½″
No. 2	1¼″	3″
No. 3	1¾″	3″
Rayo	2¼″	2⅝″
Rochester	2⅜″	2⅝″
Alladin	1 25/32″	2⅝″

Chimney heights range from 3½″ to 14″. Chimney bulge measurements from 1⅝″ to 5⅛″

You can use up to 75-watt bulbs in chimneys—with higher wattages, you run the risk of cracking the glass.

Supplies needed to electrify an oil lamp without a chimney

Wiring an oil lamp with a harp

When you want to electrify an oil lamp without reusing the chimney, you'll need a different conversion kit. For this, collect the following supplies:

- brass oil-lamp adapter (No. 1 thread for this lamp)
- 1½″ threaded nipple
- 1″ neck (either threaded or unthreaded)
- round brass locknut
- socket with side hole
- harp and finial
- cord with attached wall plug

To wire the lamp:

1. Screw adapter into neck of lamp.
2. Screw nipple into adapter.
3. Add neck.
4. Fasten down with locknut.
5. Add harp wings; screw on socket cap; thread cord into side hold; wire as in Chapter 1, Steps 9 to 14.

NOTE: If you wish to wire an oil lamp for a clip-on shade (without a harp and without a chimney), just delete the harp from your supply list and skip that step in the rewiring.

Electrifying Bracket Lamps

Bracket lamps are a standard in furnishing a bedroom or kitchen—country style in the manner of the 1890s. The ornate cast-iron, swinging-arm holders have had such continuous popularity that they are still being reproduced today.

Because glare from kerosene light was never a problem, most kerosene bracket lamps did not need shades—actually, they used mirror or shiny tin reflectors to increase the amount of light. But if you electrify a bracket lamp, you need to shield the glare of the bulb. You can do this and gain an extra bit of decorative flair by adding a student shade, gaslight shade, or petticoat shade.

NOTE: You also can use any of these treatments with the standing glass lamp, such as the one on the preceding page.

Wiring the lamp

Adding a harp to an electrified oil lamp gives you a wider choice of shades and also makes for a taller lamp—both pluses if you want to use the lamp on a living-room end table. The bell-shaped shade is antiqued shantung. Bottom diameter is 12″, top 7″, depth 8″. (A white shade photographs to look larger than it actually is.)

The antique petticoat shade rests on a chimney with a 4″ bulge. Use a candelabra bulb (with a standard base) to eliminate the glare you get from a larger bulb.

Two ways to shade a bracket lamp: supplies you need shown above, fully assembled lamps below.

To wire:

Whether you own an antique font and bracket or buy a new one, as pictured here, electrifying the lamp is easy. All you need to buy is the No. 2 prewired burner; choose one with a black cord so it will be inconspicuous against the bracket.

If you plan to add a gaslight shade, you will need a 4″ shade holder with a gallery, which slips over the prongs of the wired burner; and a satin frosted shade (4″ fitter) to slip onto the holder.

For the opal shade treatment, you need a 7″ ring that fits onto the burner and a 7″ student shade to fit it.

For both of these treatments, you need an 8½″ chimney, 3″ fitter size, 3⅝″ bulge. Use a 75-watt bulb or smaller inside the chimney.

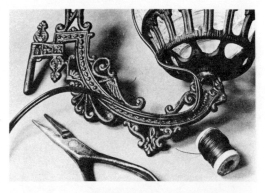

To wire the bracket: after screwing the electrified burner into the neck of the font, attach the lamp cord (with an inconspicuous black wire) to the iron bracket wherever the cord must make a sharp bend.

Supplies needed

Finished lamp with frosted globe shade

Fitting a glass lamp with a globe shade

To give your oil lamp a Gay Nineties look, convert it into a Victorian-type parlor lamp—with the addition of a frosted globe shade. For this you will need:

- converter kit (shown at base of lamp) that comes completely assembled with 4″ ring, 2⅝″ chimney holder, and prewired with socket, cord, and wall plug
- 8″ satin frosted ball shade, 4″ fitter
- 10″ chimney, 2⅝″ fitter, 3″ bulge (avoid a larger bulge, since the ball shade needs to slip over the chimney)

Converting the lamp is easy: screw the adapter and ring into the neck of the lamp; add a bulb (flame shapes work well) and chimney; set the globe on the ring, and the lamp is ready to be plugged into the wall.

Not all brass lamps have a center-draft burner. This one, with a patent date of 1893, has a flat-wick burner. To electrify it, screw in a standard No. 2 wired brass burner. The chimney (3″ fitter, 4″ bulge) has a piecrust top and a decorative etched design—a style that's still being reproduced today.

BRASS OIL LAMPS

In the 1880s, the all-metal kerosene lamp became the lamp to read by, thanks to a new invention: the round-wick, center-draft burner. The hollow in the metal base ran straight up through the font, like a hole in a doughnut, to carry air to the wick and make it burn brighter.

The burner had three parts that nested concentrically: the chimney holder, the wick tube, and, in the center, the thimble-shaped flame spreader.

Rochester was the first to introduce this burner, but many other manufacturers were quick to recognize a winner. The metal lamps you're most likely to find today, in addition to Rochester, will have such markings as Miller, Rayo, B & H (Bradley and Hubbard), Juno, Climax, Alladin.

Most of the lamps were made of brass —nickel-plated for customers willing to pay more. Today this preference is reversed: brass is in greater demand, so many dealers are stripping the nickel to expose the brass. Lamps with embossed design on the fonts are more expensive than the plain; so are the lamps with fancy, bronzed cast-iron bases.

Brass kerosene lamps are still made today—something you want to watch for if you're shopping for an original old one.

Fitting brass lamps with shades

With the brighter-than-kerosene light an electric bulb throws, the lamp will have more practical use if shaded. For this lamp with a font 5″ in diameter, you'll need a 7″ opal student shade and a 7″ tripod that slips onto the No. 2 burner

78

Same brass lamp with opal shade—turn page for list of supplies.

Supplies needed: No. 2 wired brass burner, 7″ tripod, 7″ opal student shade, 10″ chimney.

Another variation for shading the brass lamp is to use a decorative chimney shade with panels of colorful floral bouquets (at right). For this shade (12″ in diameter, 6″ deep), we used a shorter, 8½″ chimney.

to hold the shade. You'll also need to change the 3″ fitter chimney to one with a 3⅝″ bulge—so the top of the shade can slip over it. The chimney may be anywhere from 8¾″ to 10″ high, depending on how much you want exposed at the top.

To restore a Rayo, you can find parts to keep it as a kerosene-burning lamp—with the tubular wick and center-draft burner shown at left of the lamp base. Or you can find a prewired Rayo-type burner that will turn the lamp into a bright study lamp, shown at the right of the base. In addition to these supplies, you need a 10″ opal student shade and a 10″ chimney with a 2⅝″ fitter.

The Rayo Lamp

One of the best-known names in brass lamps is Rayo. If you're shopping for an authentic model, look for the embossed name on the filler cap. Most of the Rayos you'll see in antique shops today have the plain, elliptical font on a plain brass base with pierced design around the bottom. An original Rayo has the hinged tripod on which the shade rests, as illustrated here.

Many a student at the turn of the century worked on school assignments by the light of a Rayo. It's larger than most kerosene lamps made up to that time: the font is 8″ in diameter; the lamp measures 12″ to the top of the burner and 22″ to the top of the chimney.

Close-up view of Rayo lamp base shows the pierced openings around the base. Since these holes are large enough for a lamp cord to pass through, it is absolutely unnecessary to mutilate the base by drilling a hole in it for the switch. If you prefer to electrify the lamp using the original burner, you can choose a keyless socket and use a switch on the cord.

The Student Lamp

The student lamp, currently in great demand by collectors, commands a premium price. But this lamp sold well almost from the beginning, gaining its greatest popularity in the last quarter of the nineteenth century. The advertising of the day explains why: The lamp was "suitable for any place and purpose for which good light may be desired; suitable for reading, sewing, studying." Why was it more desirable than other kerosene lamps? Because the lamp was designed so that "no shadow is cast by the lamp upon the table surface." With the font holding the oil off to one side, not underneath the burner, all the light had a clear path to the table or work surface. A tube from the font carried oil to the burner, and the bottom of the lamp was heavily weighted to keep this off-balance arrangement from tipping.

Single-burner lamps were followed by double (two-burner) lamps, with the oil font in the center. Singles were also designed for wall sconces, doubles for pull-down ceiling fixtures.

The earliest student lamps were fitted with cone-shaped shades, usually of metal. But most student lamps were sold with the dome-shaped glass student shades, 7″ or 10″ in diameter. Most of the 7″ shades on the early lamps were white opal glass.

The chimney for a student lamp is considerably narrower than chimneys on other kerosene lamps; and it is straight up and down, with an enlargement at the bottom where it fits over the burner.

In 1900 you could buy a single student lamp in brass for $3.50. Today you can forget the decimal point if you're buying one in prime condition.

The list of supplies you need for electrifying a student lamp is short:

- threaded pipe 6¼″ long for this lamp
- palnut
- candelabra socket
- gold transparent lamp cord with molded-on plug
- fine brass wire

The straight-up-and-down design of the chimney limits the size of the bulb—you can use a 35-watt gas-flame bulb or a 40-watt candelabra bulb.

82

This brass student lamp measures 20″ from base to top of carrying ring. To keep its high value as an antique, it has been electrified without drilling a hole in the brass. Transparent gold cord blends with the brass color; it's hardly noticeable when drawn through holes in the vent cap and snugged against the oil tube with brass wire.

Step 1

Before you take the lamp apart, mark with a grease pencil the two holes in the vent cap that are directly under the arm.

Step 2

Unscrew vent cap from bottom, and lift burner and shade ring from top.

Cut a piece of threaded lamp pipe the length of the spiral air tube plus ¼". Screw palnut to bottom of the lamp pipe —it's just the right size to double as a washer and a hex nut. (Picture shows candelabra socket where it will be after wiring; the small socket fits snugly into the top opening.)

84

Step 3

Split the lamp cord the length of the pipe, plus enough extra so you can thread a single wire into each of the marked vent holes; then thread the lamp cord through the lamp pipe, up to the socket. Push lamp pipe up through spiral air tube. Wire socket as for candelabra on page 55. Cover socket with cardboard insulator.

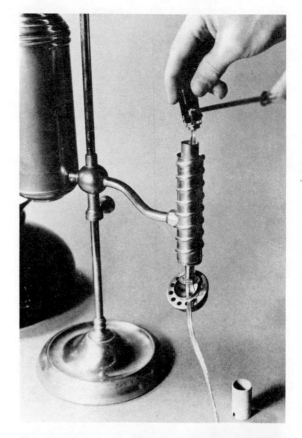

Step 4

Raise palnut and lamp pipe so you can screw the socket onto top of pipe. Tighten assembled pieces by screwing palnut. Now screw vent cap onto bottom. Attach loose lamp cord to pipe arm with brass wire. (Do not wire cord to upright standard—it needs to be free so you can raise and lower the lamp by a twist of the knob.)

Brass Lamps Ad Infinitum

There are many other styles of brass lamps you will come across when shopping the antique market for period lighting. By now, you're so experienced in rewiring, you will be able to tell, just by looking at the base, what supplies you will need! Here are a few examples.

A prize find would be this ship's light. The oil font is on a hinged base—no matter how rocky the boat, the burner will swivel into a level position.

TO ELECTRIFY: Use a No. 2 adapter and socket with a side opening, just as you did for the glass lamp converted to a harp lamp (page 75); except this time you omit the harp and add a brass-brushed opaque clip-on shade.

A ship's light maintains an even balance whether it stands on a table (above) or hangs on the wall (below).

86

This pair of ornate brass lamps mounted on marble bases lights the marble-topped Victorian dressing table most appropriately. Each lamp has been electrified with a No. 2 adapter—just as for the captain's lamps— and topped with a vinyl hexagonal clip-on shade.

This small brass whale-oil lamp makes an ideal accent lamp for a bookshelf, when electrified. To do it, use a No. 1 adapter, nipple, 1″ neck, locknut, and socket with a side hole. The clip-on shade is covered with a Williamsburg fabric design. Be sure to store the old wick top in a safe place —you may decide to display the lamp in its original state at some future time.

Opal-glass oil font has an embossed feather and fleur-de-lis design, once highlighted with gold paint that has worn off with age. Original shade probably repeated this design. Adapter is wired so that both font and shade light up. For lamp designs of this period, the shade should be larger than the base—here, a 10″ shade for the 8″ base.

REWIRING LATE-VICTORIAN PARLOR LAMPS

The decorative excesses of the Gay Nineties did not miss lamps. Designs for kerosene lamps became unbelievably flamboyant. China painters, in demand to decorate ceramics and porcelains with one-of-a-kind floral designs, were equally enthusiastic about painting huge cabbage roses and woodland scenes on lamp shades and bases. Not all were well done; there were good and bad painters in those days too.

American manufacturers advertised their ornate offerings as parlor lamps. In the shops today, they're known as Gone With the Wind lamps, because the movie sets were decorated with them (though historically, that's incorrect—the Civil War predated these lamps by twenty years).

Anyhow, these lamps have been much in vogue three times: when they were first designed, when the movie brought them out of attics, and right now because of increased interest in restoring homes of the late-Victorian period.

The lamps that still have original globes to go with the matching bases are rare indeed. Collectors pay top dollar for them. Most of today's matched sets have globes newly painted to match the bottoms—even these command high prices. But bases without tops are still reasonably priced and widely available. You can rewire and restore them—with a new globe, or, for better reading light, with a modern harp and shade.

When scouting shops or bidding at auctions, watch for two different types of fonts: 1. A font that actually holds the oil, fitted with a flat-wick burner. 2. A vase, often urn-shaped, with a brass oil pot or font inside suspended from the neck of the vase. This oil pot usually has

Lamp before: We found this lamp at auction —opal-glass font with flat-wick burner. Someone had replaced the original shade with this opal shade, which, though old, was too small for this base.

a center-draft burner; it usually sits in another brass receptacle, which has holes bored in the bottom to provide ventilation for the center draft. Both types are supported on low, ornate metal bases.

We picture examples of both the oil-font and vase-type parlor lamps and show how easy it is to electrify either one—several different ways.

89

Wiring Victorian flat-wick lamp

Step 1

To electrify: Use a 3-way wired oil-lamp converter that fits the No. 2 neck of the lamp. This adapter is wired for a light in the font—use a 7-watt bulb. The 3-way socket operates the two lights separately or both at the same time.

Step 2

Slip a 10″ ring onto the electrified burner, add a 10″ chimney with a 3″ fitter (3⅝″ bulge), then rest the 10″ opal-glass student shade on the ring.

If you top it with a globe shade, the same lamp will give an entirely different effect in the room. Use the same 3-wire converter that has a standard socket for light inside the globe and a candelabra socket for a 7-watt light for the font. Add a 4″ fitter ring with a pierced brass gallery to hold the 10″ opal globe. (A 10″ globe takes a 10″ chimney if you wish 1″ showing above the top; a 12″ chimney if you prefer 3″ showing.)

This Victorian vase lamp is fitted with an oil pot that sets into the top of the glass vase, which is attached to an ornate brass base. It's decorated with pink to deep red flowers on a turquoise background. The oil pot has a center-draft burner.

Wiring a round-wick vase lamp

Some of the Victorian lamps have a brass oil pot suspended in the neck of an urn-shaped base. The pot has a round wick with a hole through the center which makes electrifying easy.

To wire: Use a keyless socket—it will sit neatly in the center of the burner. (If the socket fits loosely in the opening of the lamp you have, steady the center pipe with a rubber adapter—the same device used for bottle lamps to give a tight fit.)

To test how much lamp pipe you will need, screw the unwired socket to lamp pipe, insert through oil-pot opening, mark the spot where it comes out of the bottom plus ¼″, and cut the pipe.

Wire the socket: Screw the socket cap to pipe, and thread the lamp cord through; then wire socket as in Chapter 1, Steps 9 to 14 (except, this time, use lamp cord without the molded plug—buy a separate plug). Drop pipe through center of oil pot and fasten at the bottom with a washer and hex nut.

Finally, thread the lamp cord through one of the holes in the receptacle, bring it out from under the base, and add the plug and a cord switch for turning the lamp on and off.

Turn the page to see the finished lamp and three different suggestions for shading the base.

This photo shows the anatomy of the vase lamp: the oil pot's center-draft burner (pictured with lamp pipe through the center to show its center opening). Next to oil pot is the brass receptacle with holes drilled in the bottom. Originally for drafting of the kerosene flame, the holes permit threading lamp cord—without drilling or otherwise altering the lamp.

This photo shows the oil part wired (through the center hole) with keyless socket, short lamp pipe, washer and hex nut.

93

Silk shade

Shades for the vase lamp

The vase lamp measures 17″ from base to burner; it's 9″ in diameter at the widest part. To balance this size, we topped it with an 11″ opal globe shade and added a 14″ chimney. A good china painter can duplicate the vase design on the globe; it will more than triple the value of the lamp. Or you can have the globe sprayed to avoid the sharp contrast of white against the dark base. Choose a color that matches the base, shading it dark around top and bottom, feathering into a lighter tone around the middle.

You get a better light to read by, however, if you top the Victorian vase lamp with a regular lampshade. Also, it's easier to deal with in decorating today's home.

It's easy to fit the lamp with a shade. Simply use a harp that screws onto the top of the socket (shown with the lamp at right). Then you decide: a bell-shaped silk shade for the living room, or a cone-shaped opaque shade for the family room or den?

Opal globe shade

Opaque shade

95

Glass canister filled with shells makes an attractive lamp base that's easy to wire, using the pitcher-lamp adapter kit (or equivalent supplies). Socket fastens to adjustable brass stem with a weighted base which you plant inside the canister (or pitcher). Sand and shells hide the weights and stem and help keep it centered in the canister.

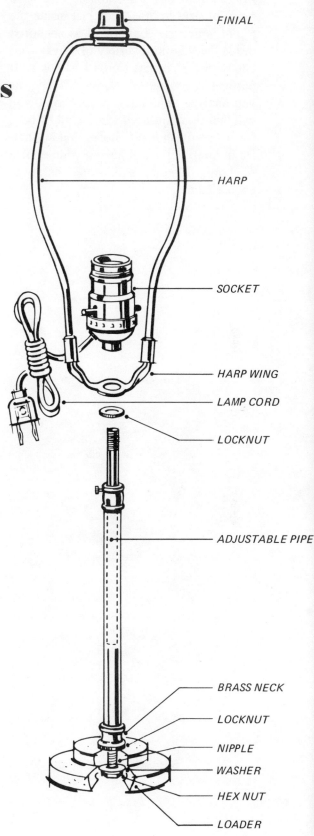

FINIAL

HARP

SOCKET

HARP WING

LAMP CORD

LOCKNUT

ADJUSTABLE PIPE

BRASS NECK

LOCKNUT

NIPPLE

WASHER

HEX NUT

LOADER

CHAPTER 6

FROM VASES TO LAMPS

The vase shape is one of the favorites in lamp design. Our eyes respond happily to familiar proportions, and the vase that looks so graceful filled with flowers remains graceful-looking when topped by a shade.

If you have a vase you enjoy looking at, don't keep it stashed away between bouquets. Bring it out of the cupboard and make a lamp of it—to use and admire every day.

Anyone can bore a hole in a vase to wire it. But you may not want it forever as a lamp. And if your vase has value as an antique or collectible, you certainly don't want to tamper with it. Drilling a hole in a Chinese porcelain, or even a country-style salt-glaze crock, drastically diminishes its value for collectors.

There's a better way—in fact, several ways—to anchor lamp fittings inside your vase without changing it or harming it. Photos in this chapter show you how.

The drawing at right diagrams the wiring for a vase (or pitcher) that remains open at the top—no cap to steady the lamp pipe. Weights (called loaders) hold the pipe upright in the center of the vase. Ask for a pitcher lamp kit; it includes the loaders and adjustable pipe so you can change the height of the shade to go with any-size vase.

This is the kit we used to wire the antique glass canister filled with shells. Dry sand makes an appropriate bed for the shells; it also covers the loaders and helps keep them from shifting.

On the pages following, you will also find directions for wiring a vase lamp

97

with a cap. Caps are available in a wide range of sizes to fit over or just inside the top of your vase. Lamp pipe is anchored inside the vase in a variety of ways—you choose the idea that works best for your particular project. And very likely, as you analyze your lamp proportions, you will find that you need some kind of base for it—to finish it off. Stores that specialize in lamp parts will have a wide choice of brass, marble, and wood bases to choose from.

SUPPLIES YOU WILL NEED

- socket with side outlet
- harp and finial
- nipple, 1½" long
- washer
- hex nut
- 2 knurled brass locknuts
- adjustable lamp pipe
- 2 loaders, 2" and 3" diameter
- lamp cord with molded plug

OPTIONAL ITEMS

- brass cap to fit vase opening (sizes range from 1½" to 7", in ⅛" gradations)
- brass neck, 1"
- wood base

ASSEMBLING A VASE LAMP WITHOUT A CAP

(follow these directions for pitcher, too)

Step 1

Screw a hex nut onto one end of the 1½" nipple. Slip a washer on top of the nut.

Step 2

Slip the two loaders over nipple and tighten with a round locknut.

Step 3

Screw adjustable brass stem assembly over the nipple. Adjust stem so it extends approximately 2" above the top of your vase. Thread second locknut over stem.

Step 4

Slip harp wings onto stem, screw on socket cap, and thread cord through side opening. Wire socket as illustrated in Chapter 1, Steps 9 to 14. Set the assembled lamp into the vase; add shade.

Pour dry sand into the bottom of the container to a depth of 5" to 6"—to keep the assembled lamp from shifting back and forth. Also use dry sand if mouth of the vase is too small to take the weights.

WIRING A VASE LAMP WITH A CAP

Light thrown on redware lamp with an open top emphasized the chips around the top of the vase. The solution: add a cap to cover the chips and a neck to raise the shade.

When you shop for a cap to fit over the top of the lamp, also pick up the adapter you need: a toggle bolt with extra-long, plastic-tipped arms. Opened wide, the toggle has a spread of 5"—enough to wedge it firmly inside most vases. The toggle kit includes the nipple and coupling with side hole for the cord outlet. This coupling also doubles as a neck.

Toggle-bolt adapter

If you can't find the toggle-bolt adapter or if it's not wide enough, make your own adapter from a metal crossbar threaded in the center hole for lamp pipe, and use a long nipple (about 6" or so). Screw the metal strap and locknut to the bottom of the nipple. Slip this assembly into the vase, straighten it, and add cap and lockwasher; then screw the neck onto the nipple, tightening it so the cap fits securely. Screw a ¾" nipple into the top of the neck, and add harp wings and wired socket with a side hole.

99

Adapter made with a
metal crossbar

Finished vase lamp with a cap

Lamp or flower holder? You can have it both ways. When flowers wilt, the matching vase is easily "corked up" to return for lamp duty. While adding necessary height, the turned-wood platform also emphasizes the silvered finish of the mercury glass. And a pleated fabric shade is appropriately fragile-looking, to top off this truly distinctive lamp.

If the vase is fragile (like this one, of mercury glass) and if it has a small neck, you can wire it as you would a bottle lamp. Slip a series of rubber adapters in graduated sizes over a long nipple, and shape them to fit the opening. Slip the cap over the nipple, and secure with a locknut. Add neck, ½″ nipple, harp wings, and wired socket.

Rubber adapters are also used to convert this Chinese cinnabar vase, but the cap is different. Instead of clamping over the rim of the vase, it fits snugly inside, below the rim. Finished lamp is raised to a better height on a carved Chinese base, in black to set off rich red of the vase.

A low, squatty urn can be boosted up to lamp height by placing it on a stack of bases. This pottery vase sits on a brass base, repeating the brass of the cap, which in turn sits on a black wood base 2″ thick.

This platform lamp displays a golden, moon-gazing rabbit—a copy of a Japanese museum piece. Oval base works best for this figure; it's topped with an oval shade of fine linen over vinyl.

CHAPTER 7

WIRING A PLATFORM DISPLAY LAMP

A lighted stage for your treasures—that's what a platform lamp is. You can make one easily (kits are available) and use it to display a precious figurine or a sparkling chunk of amethyst—or anything else you want to show off in a warm circle of lamplight. What's more, you can change your display whenever you find a new treasure: an iridescent sea shell, an amusing wood carving, or even an arrangement of garden flowers.

This kind of flexibility is different from drilling some object in order to wire it—when you convert the object itself into a lamp base. In a platform lamp, the decorative object is beautifully displayed —but never harmed. So if you've been hesitating about turning some collector's prize into a lamp, this is how you can do it without ruining it.

The bent brass stem makes this staging possible. Fastened to the back of a wood platform, this stem carries the wiring up behind the object on display; then it bends to bring the socket and shade forward, centered over the platform.

The bent brass stem in the kit is adjustable so that if you change displays, you can raise or lower the shade as necessary. The wood platforms come in round, oval, or rectangular shapes. These kits are available in hardware and electrical-supply shops and in mail-order, department, and variety stores.

If your platform lamp will have a permanent display, you may prefer to buy a piece of bent lamp pipe—threaded on both ends—in the height you need for your figurine or object. And for fine por-

celains, you may also prefer a decorative brass base. These are available in electrical-supply departments or shops that specialize in lamp parts.

SUPPLIES YOU WILL NEED

- socket
- harp and finial
- adjustable figurine lamp pipe; it's curved so the shade is centered over the item displayed, can be adjusted from 10″ to 15″ in height, and comes complete with brass neck at base
- hex nut
- 2 knurled brass locknuts
- brass washer
- brass lockwasher
- nipple, about ¼″ longer than thickness of the base
- lamp cord with molded plug
- wooden display base with a hole for lamp rod drilled near back edge (see Step 1, page 105)

STEPS IN ASSEMBLING DISPLAY LAMP

Prepare the base several days before you assemble the lamp. Sand the wood with the grain until you have a satin-smooth finish; use extra-fine sandpaper. Finish the wood according to your preference: leave it natural and wax, paint, stain, or antique. Let dry thoroughly before assembling.

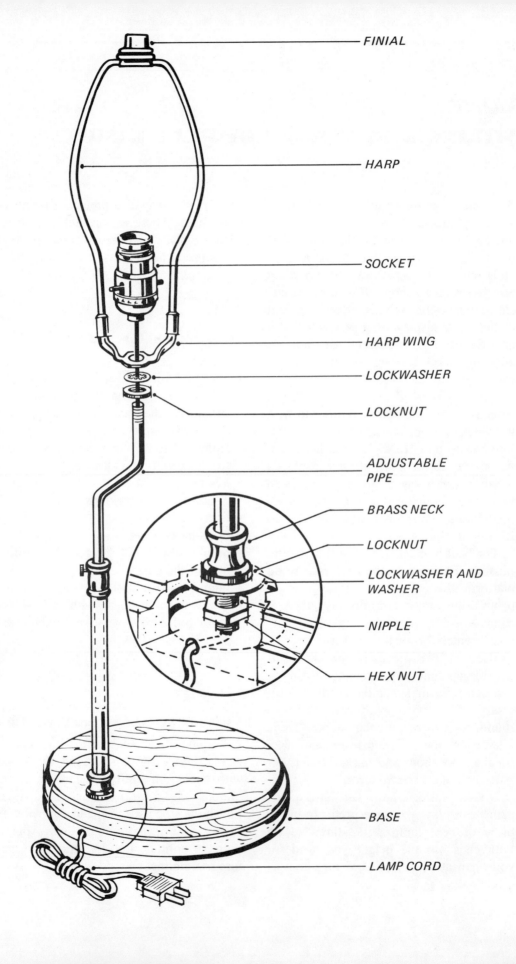

FINIAL

HARP

SOCKET

HARP WING

LOCKWASHER

LOCKNUT

ADJUSTABLE PIPE

BRASS NECK

LOCKNUT

LOCKWASHER AND WASHER

NIPPLE

HEX NUT

BASE

LAMP CORD

Step 1

Screw hex nut to one end of nipple; slip on a washer and a lockwasher; insert nipple into lamp rod hole from bottom of base.

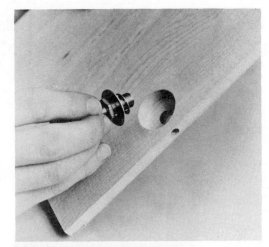

Step 2

Screw a brass locknut to nipple on top of base; then screw on the brass neck that serves as a coupling between adjustable pipe and nipple. Tighten hex nut with pliers.

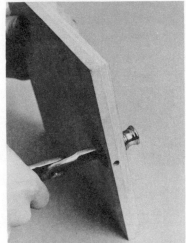

Step 3

Thread lamp cord sideways through the lamp-cord hole and up the pipe hole. Then thread it through the adjustable rod —it's easiest if you thread it through the bottom half and then the top before you put both pieces together. Screw the lamp rod into neck at the base.

Screw a round locknut to top of rod, slip on harp wings, and screw on socket cap. Wire socket as shown in Chapter 1, Steps 9 to 14.

After you add the harp, shade, and finial, set the item you wish to display on the platform and adjust the rod to the proper height; tighten screw with pliers. To prevent stripping the screw head, cover it with a piece of cloth before you use the pliers.

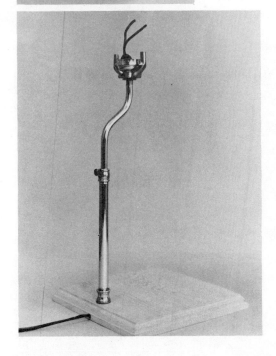

Plants prefer light. To keep them happy away from the window, place them under lamplight. This potted plant set in a copper vase rests on a round platform under a linen shade—an attractive accent light for any buffet table.

A fine porcelain figurine is suitably mounted on a filigree brass base—and requires a dressy shade such as this bell shape covered with a sheer embroidered fabric trimmed with a decorative braid. The figurine is hollow and has a hole in the bottom, so you can use a figurine toggle to secure it to the base.

106

A lamp under a lamp. An antique Chinese wedding lamp in blue-and-white pottery sits on a square wood base, painted blue to match the design. Drum shade is of pleated vinyl.

Apothecary jar

CHAPTER 8

WIRING CERAMIC LAMPS

Of all the people who come to ceramic workshops, the most satisfied are those who've made lamps. Many people decide to fire and glaze their own lamp bases after looking in vain for just the right color or design shape to match their *décor*. So why not work on a shape or figurine that pleases you? Color and glaze it precisely as you want it? And then wire it yourself! The job is so easy, it's a shame to turn it over to someone else.

You may find your ceramic shop has in stock everything you need for wiring your lamp: harps, sockets, even lamp shades in sizes to fit the bases you choose from the school's supply of molds or greenware. But even if the shop or school doesn't stock wiring supplies, the items you need to wire a ceramic lamp are easily available in hardware, mail-order, variety, or electrical-supply stores. What you save by doing the wiring yourself will be matched by your satisfaction in seeing the job through from clay to lamp plug.

In this chapter, we show some examples of popular lamp-base shapes available in ceramic studios. We list the supplies you need for each lamp and summarize the steps for wiring. If you need to see any of these steps illustrated, refer to Chapter 1.

APOTHECARY-JAR BASE

The apothecary jar with a hole drilled near the bottom for the cord is one of the all-time favorite shapes for lamp bases. Fruit and flower decal on white background makes it a decorative asset in any room. Gold bands trim the jar; the drum shade, shantung over vinyl, is also edged in gold. Lamp is 21″ tall.

To wire the apothecary lamp, you will need:

- 3″ nipple
- felt washer (not essential, but good to use between metal and china)
- Metal washer
- hex nut
- 1¼″ check ring
- round brass locknut
- 1″ neck
- socket
- harp and finial
- lamp cord with molded plug

To wire:

1. Slip felt washer, then metal washer, over bottom of nipple and screw on hex nut.
2. Insert top of nipple through neck of lamp base—from the inside.
3. Slip check ring over top of nipple; secure with round locknut.
4. Screw on neck, and add harp wings and socket cap. Bring cord through side hole in base and up through nipple; wire socket following Steps 9 to 14, Chapter 1.
5. Add harp, shade, and finial.

GINGER-JAR BASE

The ginger jar is another popular shape for lamp-base design. It is often molded as three separate pieces: lid, jar, and base. While still in greenware stage, the pieces are drilled with holes for wir-

Ginger jar

Candlestick base. Both of these ceramic lamps are molded from the same design, derived from old Italian carved-wood candlesticks. You can see that the mold for the small lamp is the same as the center section in the tall lamp. The small lamp is 15″ to the top of its white, pleated, clip-on shade; the other lamp is 34″ over all. Intended for bedroom use, the shorter, boudoir lamp has a ceramic glaze of high-gloss turquoise, which looks very clean and crisp. The taller lamp base is stained dark green—a dull finish more appropriate for living room or study. Large, drum-shaped, burlap shade requires a harp.

ing: one in the top of the lid, one in the bottom of the jar, and two in the base (center, and side). Lamp pipe runs the full length from base to lid, holding the pieces securely together (see opposite page for steps in wiring—same as for candlestick lamps). The "antiqued" finish applied to jar is a beige stain stippled over a white background. Design could be decal, but this jar is decorated with a hand-painted butterfly-and-wisteria design. Over-all height is 22″.

CANDLESTICK BASE

To wire each of these lamps, you will need:

- lamp pipe—long enough to extend from recessed base (see detail with small lamp) to socket cap
- felt washer
- metal washer
- hex nut
- brass cap for small lamp
- check ring for tall lamp
- round brass locknut
- 1″ neck
- harp and finial for tall lamp only
- lamp cord with molded plug

To wire:

1. Slip felt washer, then metal washer, onto bottom of pipe. Screw on hex nut.
2. Insert pipe through bottom of lamp to top; slip cap (or check ring) over top of pipe, and secure with round locknut.
3. Add 1″ neck, then (for tall lamp only) slip on harp wings; screw on socket cap.
4. Thread lamp cord through side hole of lamp base and up the pipe; wire socket.
5. Add clip-on shade to small lamp; harp, shade, and finial to tall lamp.

FIGURINE BASE

The figurine lamp will please anyone who likes model soldiers. Greenware at left shows a slightly different pose for the Revolutionary fighter, 10″ tall, which you can attach to a separate drum base 3″ high. With this assembly, you'll have a lamp of useful height—24″ from table to top of shade. Ceramics are stained in red, white, and blue; the opaque shade is blue with trim of plain gold braid.

To wire this or any figurine lamp, you will need:

- 1″ nipple
- felt washer
- metal washer
- hex nut
- bent brass lamp pipe, threaded top and bottom—in a length so that top of figurine fits under bend
- round brass locknut
- harp and finial
- socket
- cord with molded plug

To wire:

1. Slip felt washer, then metal washer, onto nipple; screw on hex nut at bottom.

2. Slip top of nipple through hole drilled into top of drum base; secure by screwing on 1″ neck.
3. Screw bent lamp pipe into neck.
4. Screw round locknut to top of pipe; add harp wings and screw on socket cap.
5. Thread lamp cord through side hole in drum base and up the lamp pipe; then wire socket.
6. Add harp, shade, and finial.

Figurine lamp

Molded Christmas tree

CHRISTMAS TREE

When this molded ceramic Christmas tree is lighted, it looks as if there were tiny candles shining from each branch. The second picture shows you where the light comes from: a tubular bulb and socket wired into the separate ceramic base. In the greenware stage, each tree branch is drilled so that tiny plastic "candles" can be set into the holes. The finished tree, glazed in bright green and frosted with "snow," is 24" tall.

It is the easiest of all lamps to wire; here's what you need:

- 1" nipple
- felt washer
- metal washer
- socket—use a keyless socket with insulated cardboard covering; it costs less than metal-sheathed socket
- lamp cord with molded plug
- cord switch
- tubular picture-light bulb—clear if plastic candles are multicolored. Can use colored tube lights if all candles are of one color.

To wire:

1. Slip a felt washer, then the metal washer, onto the nipple; screw on hex nut.
2. Slip top of nipple through center hole in base and screw socket to it.
3. Thread lamp cord through side hole in base and up through the nipple. Wire socket and cover with insulator sleeve.
4. Add cord switch (see page 58).
5. Screw in bulb and set tree on top of base.

ACCENT LIGHT

This small accent light—when you take it apart with your eyes—looks like nothing more than a cylinder vase and a bare round light bulb. Glazed in smart-looking black, the base is 8" tall, 3½" in diameter. It's easy to rig, because the mold anticipates the wiring. There's a deep recess in the top, enough to hide the neck of the 5″ bulb as well as the socket. Bottom is also recessed and both top and bottom are drilled with holes so that you can secure nipple and socket fittings.

To wire, you will need:
- 4″ nipple—or a length that extends ¼″ above and below top and bottom openings
- round locknut
- felt washer
- metal washer
- hex nut or round locknut for top of nipple
- candle socket with cardboard insulator
- lamp cord with molded plug
- cord switch
- 5″ round bulb, inside-white finish

To wire:
1. Slip washers (felt and metal) on bottom of nipple and screw on hex nut.
2. Insert nipple through bottom hole in vase and up through top hole; screw locknut onto top.
3. Thread lamp wire through side hole in vase and up nipple through the top; wire socket before screwing it onto nipple; cover socket with cardboard insulator.
4. Add cord switch (see page 58); screw in bulb, and light.

PLASTER BASE

If you're interested in plaster crafts instead of ceramics, you will find a large assortment of molds suitable for cast lamp bases. Wiring steps are similar to ceramics, with this important difference: You insert lamp pipe through the center of the mold before you pour. The pipe is positioned so that top and bottom threads are accessible for screwing on socket, couplings, nipples, or whatever is needed to finish the lamp. (See completed lamp on page 165.)

113

Accent light

Plaster base showing center lamp pipe exposed

Converted gas table lamp

CHAPTER 9

RESTORING TURN-OF-THE-CENTURY LAMPS

GAS LAMPS

Gaslight named an era that has been, until recently, virtually ignored except by nightclubs and moviemakers. While the use of gas lamps and fixtures was concurrent with kerosene (both of them preceding electricity), gaslight was mostly restricted to townspeople and affluent houses.

In the last half of the nineteenth century, the gaslight era produced some of the most graceful and beautifully crafted lighting fixtures of all time. And the restoration of turn-of-the-century townhouses in today's city centers has stirred up a new interest in these designs.

Though gaslight was widely used by 1850, it is not likely you'll find fixtures from the earliest years. The most available—and affordable—will be those still being made twenty years after Edison invented the first practical incandescent bulb. Tiffany, universally known for his Art Nouveau electric lamps, also featured gas and kerosene lamps in his line. So did Sears; their 1900s mail-order catalogs picture all three types of lighting.

When we talk of the gaslight era, first thoughts go to chandeliers and wall sconces. Portable table lamps are less well known. They were styled with heavy bases and columnar pipes; a long rubber hose connected lamp to wall outlet.

Most of these lamps are easy to convert to electricity. The electric socket in the lamp at left, for example, fits the same threading that once held the gas jet. By removing the stopcock at the base, you have a more-than-ample opening for

Not yet electrified, this gas lamp still has its stopcock. The original chimney and frosted globular shade with cut design add much to its value. Chimney is typically tall and thin (8″×1¾″), frosted on the lower 1½″. To electrify, remove stopcock and wire burner with candelabra socket, following directions for gas wall sconce (page 126).

Electrified gas lamp with stopcock removed and lamp cord threaded through. Glass shade is a collectible but not original for this lamp.

This Art Nouveau lamp is a signed Tiffany, though it is more restrained than most of his designs. The simple base, like a plant stem, is topped with his "turtle" lamp shade. Art pottery displayed with the lamp is typical of designs prized by collectors of this period.

lamp cord. The original cased-glass shade sits on its original four-pronged ring holder.

ART NOUVEAU AND ART DECO ELECTRIC LAMPS

Collectors interested in early electric lamps split into two camps: Those who look for (and can afford to buy) original lamps and fixtures—in this field, the Tiffany name leads all the rest. And those who are interested in collecting the iridescent art glass shades. If signed by Tiffany, Steuben, Quezal, or Durand, the shades are real finds to be prized; they are often displayed on a shelf or in a lighted cabinet, while lesser shades are collected with the intention of using them as decorative lights (see page 156).

Historically the shades are important, because they mark an important change in lamp design. Electric light was the first light to hang down; all flame lights are up lights. Naturally, just as soon as people got over the novelty of the new bulb, designers started to work on shielding the glare. All this happened in a design period now referred to as Art Nouveau. The Art Nouveau designs were fluid, sinuous, sensuous—like long hair flowing gracefully over a woman's shoulders. This is the era when Tiffany designed his famous stained-glass lamp shades in such patterns as wisteria and dragonfly.

Rewiring a genuine Tiffany lamp is not covered in this book. Tiffany made over five hundred different designs, many with individually styled wiring and socket systems; rewiring or repairing them is a job for an expert. When they sell at auction, lamps of such value are in perfect working order. Today, one of his lamps may command a five-figure price —and no one winces.

But the myriads of Tiffany-*type* lamps do lend themselves to the problem-solv-

116

ing ideas you'll find in this book. Copies of true Tiffany designs, copies of lamps by other designers of the same period, plus other designs inspired by the old lamps—all are available under the Tiffany-type umbrella.

The word "art" was often part of the individual design name for patterns in art glass and art pottery during this period— under the umbrellas Art Nouveau and Art Deco.

Art Deco came in on the opposite swing of the design pendulum, with geometric flower designs and zigzag lighting effects only slightly softened by the curved lines of leaping gazelles and dancing women in long skirts. Recent museum shows are partly responsible for a revived interest in this period. But it's also true that Art Deco is still affordable.

An example of Art Deco lamp design. The heavy, straight lines are typical: heavy iron base, heavy metal framework in the shade, holding green glass panels.

If you yearn for an Art Nouveau lamp but haven't found one in your price bracket, it's possible to assemble the look from new components. Lamp at left is an example; shade and base are available separately. Curved to look like flower petals, the shade's glass panels are held in a decorative metal framework. Shade is equipped with a metal strap so that it fits onto the finial stud of a table lamp; or it can be wired up as a hanging lamp (see page 157).

117

You may find a good buy in an old shade because the base is missing. All you need to give it useful life is a new base, like the one shown with the all-new lamp above. This base is equipped with an adjustable shade riser that can be raised or lowered according to the size of your shade.

Certain old shades have open tops; originally they hung from a round metal disk that was part of the lamp-base design. You can easily adapt such a shade to fit a modern fixture. Clamp two lamp caps over the hole; hold them together with a nipple, adding washers and locknuts on each side. Use a reducer on the nipple to fit it onto a lamp finial stud. Or use the shade as a hanging light by attaching a loop to the nipple.

If you find an old lamp base such as the Art Deco type shown here—but no shade—keep your eyes open for one that looks good with it. We found a frosted shade with a hand-painted fruit design; but even a plain tam o' shanter opal shade would do. Or you might consider ordering a custom-made shade from a craftsman who does stained glass.

Art pottery—highly desirable in today's *décor* —brings top dollar from collectors. Many of the vases make stunning lamp bases and you need have no hesitancy about converting one; you'll not destroy its value if you don't drill a hole in it. The Grueby vase pictured here, with hand-modeled leaf shapes, has a dark green matte finish—typical of the designs put out by the Grueby factory in the early 1900s. It's wired with a cap and toggle kit which has a coupling with a side hole for the cord. Chapter 6 tells you how to wire this type vase.

All it takes to convert this brass wall sconce from gas to electricity is a candelabra socket, a foot of lamp cord, and a 20-cent reducing bushing. Polishing gives it the soft patina that comes with age. Blown shade with opalescent swirls is in keeping with period. See step-by-step directions on page 124.

CHAPTER 10

DIMMER SWITCHES AND WALL SCONCES

If you've never removed the plate that covers a wall switch (except possibly to paint), why not install a dimmer switch as a glamorous learning project? It's an easy way to get acquainted with the kind of wiring anyone can do.

And once you have installed a dimmer, you'll have the confidence—plus the know-how—to tackle wall lights or sconces. This knowledge should save you money in other ways. You may not need a new sconce if you can rewire and rejuvenate what you have. Or you might find some old fixture salvaged from a demolished building—a good buy if you know you can rewire it yourself and end up with something exactly right for your house.

Such electrical work is well within the province of the aspiring handyman and is gladly relinquished by the professionals. In spite of what seem like high labor costs to us, most electricians don't find it profitable to make house calls for such small jobs.

Obviously, we're not talking about your making any changes in basic house wiring or installing new outlets where there were none before. Between-the-wall wiring is for experts; but the wires you work on to change switches or wall plugs, or repair or replace sconces, are accessible—in full view in the junction box right behind the wall plate or fixture

plate. As you can see (directions follow), it's a simple, five-minute project.

But first, one important caution. Before you pick up your screwdriver, go to the control panel or fuse box and turn off the current that controls the light or outlet you'll be working on.

To find the circuit, turn on the light at the switch or sconce you want to work on. (Plug in a lamp if you're working on a wall plug.) Then switch off the circuits one by one (or remove fuses one by one) to see which one controls the outlet or fixture. When you find it, leave the circuit breaker OFF (or keep the fuse removed) until you're through with your electrical work.

Never stand on a wet floor when you're working around electrical wires—whether at the control panel or at the switch.

INSTALLING A DIMMER SWITCH

With a dimmer switch, you can dial any light level you want from full bright (for most dimmers, capacity is 600 watts) down to zero. Dimmers are worth installing just for mood control—but they also save you money. As you soften the light you also cut down on wattage used, and bulbs last longer, too, when burned below capacity.

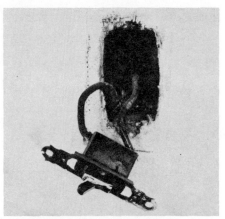

Step 1

Cut off circuit breaker (or remove the fuse) that controls the switch. Remove old switch plate by taking out the two screws. Then remove the screws that hold switch in junction box. Pull old switch out of the box—wires are stiff and you may have to use a bit of force. Disconnect wires from switch.

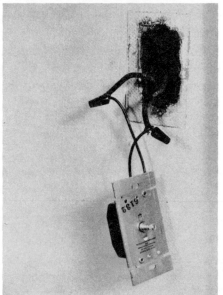

Step 2

With wire nuts, connect the two wires from dimmer switch to the two wires in junction box. To do this: hold exposed wire ends (one from wall, one from dimmer) close together, fit the plastic wire nut over the end, and twist clockwise. (See page 190.)

Step 3

Push connected wires into junction box, then seat dimmer in the box. Use the two screws that came with the unit to hold it securely in place.

Step 4

Replace the face plate over the dimmer unit with the two screws. Push dimmer knob onto control shaft. Turn the power back on, push control knob in, and dial the brightness you want. Push knob in again to turn the lights off.

122

REWIRING A WALL SCONCE

Once you know how to put in a wall switch or a dimmer, you're ready to tackle wall lights, or sconces. Installation is exactly the same procedure: connecting the two wires on the sconce to the two wires in the junction box.

Your fixture may be new, or it may be some salvageable old relic like the one we worked on. Whether new or old, if it has a switch on the face plate, there will be four wires (not two) to connect in your installation. Our photos show you how to make this connection.

Wall sconce—before and after. Wobbly old wall sconce showed years of neglect, its once-shiny brass tarnished and spattered with paint. Nor was the chimney-type bulb a suitable choice. Restoration included cleaning and polishing, rewiring, and the addition of a gracefully shaped glass shade.

Step 1

Turn off circuit breaker (or remove the fuse) that controls the wall light. Then remove the decorative knob that holds the sconce to the junction box.

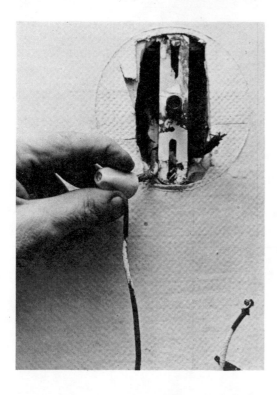

Step 2

By removing the face plate, you reveal a crossbar that holds the nipple to which the face plate was attached. Remove the wire nuts that connect the fixture wires to the outlet wires.

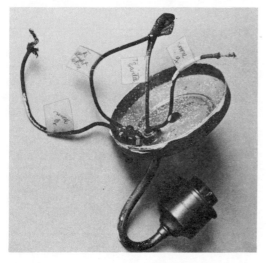

Step 3

Here's how to keep track of four wires so that you can reconnect them properly. When you detach the wires, note where each one goes and label it accordingly with tape. One wire from the sconce arm is attached to one of the outlet wires; one wire from the switch is attached to the other outlet wire. The two remaining wires—one from the sconce arm, one from the switch—are attached to each other. (After you've wired a sconce-with-switch a time or two, you won't need identifying labels any more.)

124

Step 4

Remove the socket so you can see if wires need replacing. These definitely do —they're badly frayed. You'll need two fixture wires (or you can use regular lamp wire) the same length as the old. Rewire socket following Steps 9 to 14 in Chapter 1.

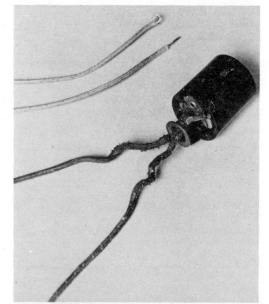

Step 5

Clean and polish the old fixture. (Soak brass parts in a half-and-half solution of ammonia and water to remove old lacquer; use extra-fine steel wool for stubborn spots; shine with a brass polish such as Simichrome.) Then thread wires of the rewired socket through chimney cup and arm of sconce; screw socket to fixture arm.

With a small wire nut, connect as labeled one switch wire to one of the new sconce wires.

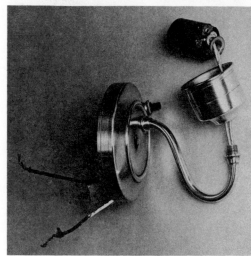

Step 6

Attach the crossbar to junction box with the two screws. Then, with a wire nut, connect the second sconce wire (as labeled) to one of the outlet wires. Connect the second switch wire to the other outlet wire. Push the two wire nuts and wires into the junction-box cavity.

Fit the sconce back over the nipple in the center of the crossbar, and screw the brass knob (now cleaned) onto the nipple end to hold the sconce securely.

Add a new glass shade and you end up with a fixture that looks good as new! (See page 123.)

WIRING A GAS SCONCE

The fixtures of the gaslight era decorated homes with a gracefulness we can admire today—and easily utilize. You might find a wall sconce, as we did, in a box of old hardware—blackened with age, but solid brass underneath and well worth the polishing. Up to now, gaslights have been somewhat overlooked by collectors, but that is beginning to change.

Gas pipe is larger than lamp pipe, so you will need a reducer to secure the sconce to the wall outlet. The threading at the flame tip, however, is the same size as lamp pipe. And in making the conversion, you will eliminate the spigot or valve that originally controlled gas flow. Here are the step-by-step directions for the sconce shown on page 120.

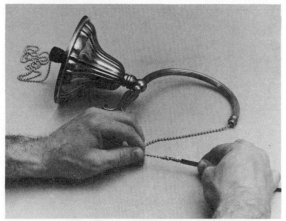

Step 1

Disassemble this gas fixture by screwing off the gas nozzle, lifting off the shade holder, and unscrewing the spigot and the decorative brass plate below the spigot. (The spigot, which controlled the gas flame, will be eliminated in the rewired fixture.)

Step 2

By itself, lamp cord will not make the sharp bend in the fixture arm. Here's how to lead it through, using beaded chain. Slink the chain through first—if it doesn't go through easily from one end, try the other end. Twist exposed wires of lamp cord onto the chain. To grip firmly, twist half the wires in one direction, half in the opposite direction.

Step 3

Draw lamp cord through the arm: pull the chain with one hand, and gently feed the wire (by pushing) into the other end.

126

Step 4

Place the lamp-shade holder and then the decorative plate over the end of the arm; screw a locknut to hold them in place (fortunately, the threading is the same size as lamp pipe). Screw a candelabra socket onto the end of the arm, and wire—as in Chapter 1, Steps 9 to 14.

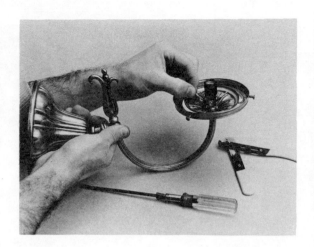

Step 5

Gas pipe is larger than that used in electric fixtures. In order to make the gaslight fixture fit the nipple in the junction box, screw a headless brass reducing bushing (¼-M×⅛-F) into the gas outlet (see Glossary for explanation of sizes).

Step 6

Feed the wire from the sconce through the nipple and pull it out of the junction box, one wire to each side of the crossbar. Connect each wire to an outlet wire —with a wire nut, as for the previous sconce.

Push wires into the cavity, then screw the fixture onto the nipple. Push the cap against the wall and fasten to the arm with the setscrew at the top of the cap.

Add an antique or new gaslight shade onto the shade holder to complete the light.

127

This candle-type chandelier of heavy metal is an old one—a style popular in the golden-oak era. Refurbished and rewired, it hangs compatibly over any of today's country-style furnishings, be they English, Spanish, or U.S.A.-rural in feeling. You can change the character—and the lighting effect—of the chandelier by changing bulbs, adding clip-on shades, or wiring with regular, rather than adjustable, candle sockets (see photos following; also photos in next chapter).

CHAPTER 11

CHANDELIERS AND OTHER CEILING FIXTURES

If you can install a wall sconce, you can also connect a chandelier—the wiring is the same.

But pick a time when you have a helper; you need someone to hold up the fixture while you are fussing with the wiring; some fixtures are quite heavy. It's foolhardy to try a balancing act while you're standing on a ladder. And do use a sturdy ladder, safely positioned.

Before you begin, collect all the supplies you will need for the type fixture you're installing. Then—most important —go to the fuse box or circuit breaker to **cut off the electricity to the ceiling outlet.**

Ceiling outlet boxes are bigger than most wall outlets. In newer houses, they are square with cut corners (upper right), and as deep as the rectangular wall boxes. In an old home, you're more likely to find a round and shallow box with a center stud (lower right). This style box requires one extra item: a hickey. Otherwise, the basic wiring is the same as for the wall sconces.

If you have double switching (two wall switches that control the same fixture), you will see more than two wires in the box when you uncover it. But you need be concerned only with the two wires that connect to the fixture. You can ignore the other wires.

Photos that follow show you, first, how to install a simple ceiling fixture. Then you'll see how to rewire a five-light chandelier and how to wire it into the ceiling box. Whether your fixture is a three-, four-, or six-light chandelier, you'll rewire it the same way.

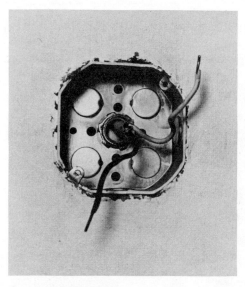

Square ceiling outlet

Round ceiling outlet

Finally, there are directions for rewiring a hollow-arm, one-light fixture with two single wires (fixture wire), and how to electrify a hanging kerosene library lamp.

DISH-TYPE CEILING FIXTURE

Almost every home needs a simple, flat ceiling fixture in some room of the house—bedroom, bath, utility room. You'll choose it if your ceiling is too low for a hang-down fixture or if you use the ceiling light only occasionally and wish to keep it as inconspicuous as possible. This type fixture is extremely easy to install, and just as easy to shop for since everything you need usually comes pre-packed in an inexpensive kit:

Parts needed to install dish-type ceiling fixture

- metal canopy that fits over outlet box
- snap-in double fixture socket
- bent-glass diffuser
- cap nut with two felt washers

To wire:

1. With cupped side of canopy toward ceiling, thread wires of fixture socket through center opening and snap socket in place.

   Connect white fixture wire to white wire in ceiling box; then connect black fixture wire to black ceiling wire. Use wire nuts.

   Thread the two screws into the two ears on the outlet box.

Canopy wired to ceiling outlet

2. Slip the canopy over the screw heads and twist slightly so screw heads slide into the narrow slots of screw holes. Tighten screws to secure canopy against ceiling.

   Lamp the fixture with bulbs (check information in kit for recommended wattage). Then you're ready to add the bent-glass diffuser: slip felt washer over the nipple at bottom of fixture; add diffuser, another felt washer, and secure with cap nut.

Canopy securely fastened to ceiling outlet

Reading this chapter should convince you to grab a funky old chandelier if you like its style. People who don't know how easy it is to rewire fixtures pass up good buys—bargains at auction or in a junk shop. Or you may have one still hanging in a house you're restoring. If the chandelier is in reasonably good condition—or if you know you can clean it up and make the necessary repairs—rest assured you can also rewire it.

We found the perfect old chandelier to demonstrate steps in rewiring. It carries the wiring on the outside of the arms, so you can see it clearly in all the photos that follow. Your find may have hollow arms—or a different number of arms—but the wiring connections will be the same, and our pictures show you how to make them. Just follow Steps 1 through 6 to take it apart, wire it, and put it back together again.

Once the chandelier itself is repaired, hanging it is a little different from putting up the simple dish-type fixture. But it's not difficult, and everything you need comes in a handy kit.

Step 1

Take the fixture apart. It's necessary if you're going to replace any sockets. Even if the sockets are in good condition, it's always advisable to check the wiring in old fixtures to make sure there are no raw wires exposed.

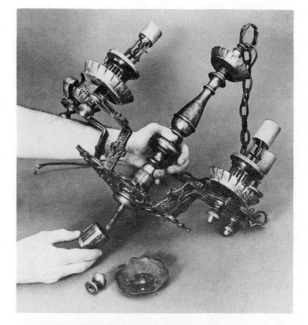

Step 2

Some fixtures have so many parts, you may not remember exactly how to fit all the loose pieces back together again. Take a minute to arrange or label parts in the order in which you remove them.

Keep going until you've unfastened the arms from the center stem unit and exposed the wire connections.

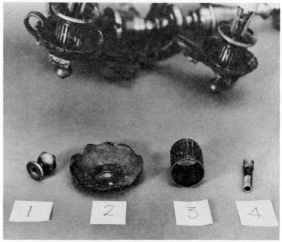

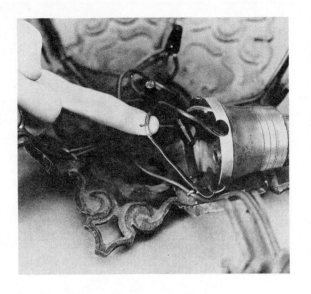

Step 3

Check the wiring carefully; this fixture had several cuts in arm wires, some more obvious than others. The cuts were caused in part by the sharp edges of the stem that fits into the center of the arm section—you'll see (in Step 6 photo) what you can do to protect cord when you rewire.

Remove old wires from arms and sockets; measure to get length needed for new wires. For this fixture we used regular lamp cord. Rewire the sockets as in Chapter 1, Steps 9 to 14. Then carry lamp cord down each arm to the center—in this fixture, the cord is snugged to arms with staple-like devices which are part of the fixture design.

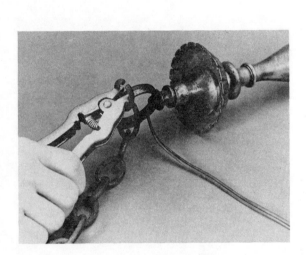

Step 4

At the other end of the central stem, open link to replace rusty chain. A chain pliers is the easy tool to use: it's designed with a nose that pries the link apart when you press the handles together.

Step 5

If wire in center stem of chandelier needs replacing, thread the new lamp cord down through the fixture stem. Cord should be long enough to weave through the chain above the stem with extra inches to wire into ceiling outlet.

In this photo, cord from center stem is being connected to cord from each of the five sockets. To do this, split all cord ends and strip each of the wire ends. Take one wire from each arm (five wires total) and one wire from the center stem: twist all six wire ends together with

a wire nut—clockwise. Repeat with remaining six wire ends. (Photo shows how we taped the last six wire ends out of the way while we worked on the first connection.)

Step 6

Set the fixture stem onto the center of the arm section, easing wire nuts and wires into the hollow part of the stem. (At this juncture, we wound our new wires with electrician's tape to protect them from being cut by sharp edges of stem.)

Finish reassembling the fixture with remaining pieces removed in Steps 1 and 2. Weave the lamp cord through the fixture chain. Cover sockets with cardboard insulators and waxlike candle covers.

HANGING THE CHANDELIER

You can buy supplies separately for hanging a ceiling fixture, but the easier way is to pick up a fixture-hanging kit—some include the canopy that covers the outlet box. These kits have everything you need to get the job done, no matter what kind of ceiling outlet you have. The kit shown here includes:

- 1½" nipple, ¼-IP
- hickey, ⅜-IP×¼-IP (see Glossary for explanation of sizes)

Parts needed to hang a chandelier

- screw-nut loop and collar ring
- crossbar tapped for ¼-IP nipple
- 2 locknuts, one threaded ¼-IP, the other ⅜-IP.

If you have the square ceiling outlet, you won't need the hickey and nuts in the prepacked kit. If you have the shallow round outlet with center stud, found in old houses, you need the hickey but not the crossbar.

The screw-nut loop and collar ring in this kit holds the canopy up on the ceiling—any canopy with a center hole 1¹⁄₁₆" in diameter.

A canopy with a ⁷⁄₁₆" center hole takes a regular loop (threaded ¼-IP). This canopy has two screw holes in the cap—it's held to the ceiling by screwing it to the crossbar.

When you are ready to connect the fixture to the ceiling outlet, pick up the canopy and fixture-hanging kit (or equivalent supplies) shown at left. Because our fixture is gray-toned metal, we used a steel canopy, also gray.

To wire into a square ceiling box:

1. Attach the top link of the chain to the screw-nut loop and collar ring. (Use chain pliers.)
2. Screw the crossbar onto the lips of the ceiling box; screw the nipple into the crossbar.
3. Thread the lamp cord through the loop, through the canopy, and through the nipple. Split end of lamp cord and strip wire ends; attach one wire to the black outlet wire, the other wire to the white outlet wire, using wire nuts (just as for previous ceiling fixture).
4. Push the wire nuts into the box. Place canopy over the outlet, screw loop onto the nipple, then screw collar over the loop to hold the canopy in place.

Attaching a chandelier to a square ceiling box

To wire fixture into an older,
stud-type outlet box:

1. Spin the ⅜-IP locknut onto the stud.
2. Screw the ⅜-IP end of hickey onto the stud, against the locknut.
3. Screw nipple into ¼-IP end of hickey and spin the ¼-IP locknut up against the hickey.
4. Thread lamp cord through the loop, canopy, and nipple, bringing it out in the U-shaped opening of the hickey; connect wires and finish installation as in Steps 3 and 4 on opposite page.

Now you can replace the fuse (or throw the circuit-breaker switch) and turn on the lights. If one candle doesn't light, it means that one of the wires from the arm has slipped out of the wire nut. In that case, turn off the electricity again and retrace the steps so you can redo the wire nut.

SHADES FOR THE CHANDELIER

You can change the character of any chandelier with shades. The white plastic pleated clip-on shades (middle right) tend to make this fixture look a little more formal—more dressed up. They also soften and spread light into the room. For more directional light onto the table surface below (and less over-all room light), try small, opaque metal shades.

To emphasize the country feeling in the coarse metal texture of this fixture, you might choose pressed-glass shades in frosted amber (bottom right). But you would have to decide on these shades before you wired the fixture. Adjustable sockets are too tall; the arms should be fitted with regular sockets in either standard or candelabra size.

The bulbs you choose can also make a difference in the looks of your chandelier —see examples in the next chapter.

135

Attaching a chandelier to a stud-type ceiling box

White plastic pleated clip-on shades

The same fixture with pressed-glass shades

If you have an old shade you like, but no fixture to go with it, look in secondhand shops or flea markets. This three-arm, one-light fixture and shade ring (with hooks for prisms) is a good choice designwise to complete the library lamp—even though it's newer than the frosted-and-cut tam o' shanter shade. Chimney has a 3″ base.

REWIRING WITH FIXTURE WIRE

When you start to rewire a fixture with hollow arms, you may find the openings are too small to take regular lamp cord. What you need is fixture wire. It's a single wire—the same size as one of the wires in the double-wire cord. While most fixture wire is rayon-covered, you can also get it plastic-covered, in brown, black, or white.

To wire:

Step 1

Take the fixture apart, remove old wires, and polish up all the brass pieces. Slink a ball chain through the openings of the arm. Then strip the end of fixture wire and twist it around the ball chain at the far end of the arm; pull the wire through the arm into the center of the fixture. (Use a generous length of wire, enough to pass through chain from base of fixture to the ceiling outlet.)

Step 2

Repeating the process, pull a second length of wire through the second arm (third arm does not get wired). Wire the socket with the two wire ends in the center of the fixture, following Steps 9 through 14, Chapter 1. Place cardboard insulator over the newly wired socket, and put the fixture back together.

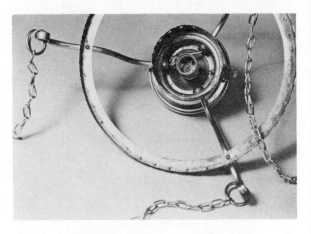

If the chain needs replacing, buy enough to cut three lengths. For this fixture, we chose a chain of "small" polished brass links—only ¾" long (most chain links are 1½").

Weave the two lengths of fixture wire through two of the three chains and through the open hooks in canopy.

Step 3

Screw crossbar onto the lips of the ceiling outlet box. Insert nipple. Wire the two fixture wires to the two wires in ceiling box, using wire nuts.

137

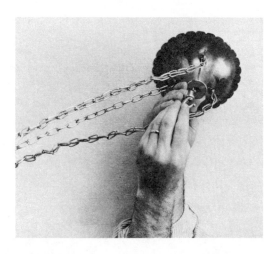

Step 4

The canopy for this fixture could be held up against the ceiling with a loop. But instead of using an ordinary loop, we wanted to install a hook so we could suspend a smoke bell over the chimney. The male hook we selected is threaded ⅛-IP, so we added a coupling to the end of the nipple to receive the hook.

And to cover up the too-large hole in the canopy, we slipped a check ring over the opening before screwing in the male hook.

A hanging oil lamp is a possession prized by owners of early-twentieth-century houses. Commonly known as a library lamp, it is ideally suited for dining-table lighting. This one has a frosted font that sits on a brass peg; the shade is of green cased glass.

The chain for the smoke bell is the "very small" size (½" links) in the same polished brass as the fixture chain (see photo, opposite page).

ELECTRIFYING A HANGING KEROSENE LAMP

It's easy to electrify a hanging kerosene fixture. All you need is a prewired oil-lamp converter to fit a No. 2 neck, wired with dark brown lamp cord to blend with the brass hardware.

To wire:

Cut off the molded plug first—you don't need it for wiring to the ceiling outlet box. Then screw the converter into the neck of the font.

The double lamp cord that comes with the converter is too large to weave through the fine chain on the fixture. To remedy this, split the cord so it can go in two directions. (The alternative is to rewire the oil-lamp converter with fixture wire.)

Start at the end where you cut off the plug. Slit the end of the cord with a sharp knife and start pulling the two plastic-coated wires apart—carefully, so as not to expose any copper.

When you get to the bottom of the font, guide one of the two wires along one brass arm, the other across the bottom of the font holder and up the other brass arm. Fasten wires to the brass frame wherever necessary to hold it snug —use the fine brass wire for this (see photo, lower left).

Carry wires along the inside of the shade ring and up the nearest chain. Fasten cord to chain with fine brass wire. Links of upper chain are larger, so cord can be woven through chain, in and out every four or five links.

Connect wires to ceiling outlet and suspend smoke ring as shown in preceding library lamp.

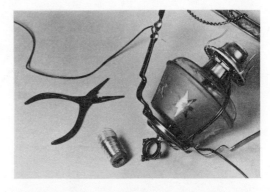

Double lamp cord split to go in two directions

Lamp cord is fastened to chain at right but is still to be fastened to chain at left.

If you are restoring an old house, take time to shop for a light fixture that goes with the period. Today's craftsmen take pride in reproducing authentic designs (below). Or you may find old fixtures to electrify—such as the two antique lanterns of a style used in the 1700s now hanging in a restored home of that period (opposite).

The handcrafted candelabra in the restored kitchen is wrought iron. The artist who crafted this fixture glued a very fine (No. 22) lamp cord to the iron arms—with epoxy—then painted wires and iron black.

Lantern above was wired with a candelabra socket; the wire runs through metal loops soldered into the corners of the lantern and out ventilation holes in the lantern cap.

Lantern at right hangs from an old wrought-iron hook. The cord exits sideways—through the hole drilled into the wooden wall above the cellar door. It plugs into a wall outlet in the stairwell.

141

Use clear bulbs when you want to make crystal chains and pendants sparkle—they also emphasize the graceful outline of this glass chandelier. Bulbs are torpedo-shaped, with candelabra-size bases.

Some decorative bulbs are available in standard base for the few fixtures with standard sockets. The torpedo shape in clear glass is a good choice for this large-scale fixture.

Round bulbs repeat the shape of the crystal balls attached to the ends of chrome rods in this ceiling-hugging fixture. Again, choose clear bulbs to maximize the sparkle.

In white glass the standard-base bulb tends to look squatty. Bulbs with candelabra bases (the three at right) look more graceful. Socket reducers make the change possible.

CHAPTER 12

LAMPING THE CHANDELIER, WALL SCONCES, AND OTHER FIXTURES

Most of us spend as much time shopping for just the right chandelier to hang over the dining-room table as for the table itself. Since the chandelier is such a conspicuous part of an over-all decorating plan, it's worth the effort.

But finding the right fixture isn't the end of shopping for light. The fixture doesn't come alive until it is properly lamped. Bulbs are, literally, the crowning touch—the jewelry for the fixture! And they should have eye appeal whether they're lighted or not. The wrong choice of bulbs can downgrade your chandelier, just as a wrong necklace can undo the perfection you pay for in an expensive gown.

If your fixture dealer is large enough to have a lighting specialist who can advise you, you're in luck. If not, it's up to you to know what to ask for; you can't depend on a clerk to lamp your chandelier correctly.

And unless you've been actively admiring other people's chandeliers or shopping for decorative lamp bulbs, you probably aren't aware of the incredible variety on the market. Only the most ordinary bulbs are stocked in supermarkets. To see what else is available, visit the stores that specialize in lighting. Look through fixture catalogs and magazines to see how designers lamp fixtures. You will be surprised at how many different ways you can simulate candle-light or gaslight, for example. And how exciting it can be, lamping a chandelier.

While it is difficult to show the quality of light on a printed page, photographs in this chapter suggest what light bulbs look best with what fixtures. They also demonstrate how easy it is to change the look of a light fixture merely by changing the light bulbs. The idea is something like accessorizing a basic black dress, or buying ties. Collect a wardrobe of light bulbs —then you can vary the lighting effect according to the seasons, the occasion, or your mood.

There are, of course, a few technicalities to keep in mind: socket sizes, finishes, shapes, colors, wattages. Information in this chapter will make you an informed shopper.

BULB BASES

Decorative bulbs come in two base sizes: candelabra and standard. The standard (or Edison) base is the familiar size used for table lamps and shielded ceiling fixtures in general use throughout the house. The candelabra base is smaller, permitting the design of smaller, more graceful-looking bulbs.

Most chandeliers—about 95 per cent of them—are fitted with candelabra sockets. So it follows that you will find the largest selection of styles and shapes in bulbs with a candelabra base. The variety, in fact, is virtually unlimited: flame-shaped bulbs, some with delicately pinched tops, some that flicker to imitate candle flames, some that look amazingly like gaslight. Also, round bulbs for makeup mirrors and sleek modern

143

fixtures, and many decorative bulbs for special occasions.

The other 5 per cent of the fixtures are purposely designed to look sturdy—bold in scale. And they look well when lamped with bulbs that have a standard socket—the larger neck is in good proportion to a wagon-wheel fixture, for instance. Or to heavy cast-metal fixtures with candle covers 1½″ in diameter. Most outdoor and post-lantern fixtures are also wired with standard sockets.

But even fixtures with standard-size sockets sometimes look better with small-necked bulbs. If this is true for a fixture you own, don't despair. You can buy a socket reducer for less than the cost of a light bulb. Then you can use standard or candelabra bulbs interchangeably.

There are two other bulb-base sizes to know about. One is the mogul socket size —an extra-large base for high-wattage bulbs. You may need this for certain floor lamps but never for fixtures. In specialty stores, you may also find bulbs that look like the candelabra size but are really designed for a different-size socket made in Europe. Read the label so you don't inadvertently pick the wrong bulb for the fixture you have. If you have a chandelier from France or Italy, you may need to look for this intermediate size.

The incandescent lamp glows and lasts because the filament burns in a vacuum. To maintain the vacuum, the glass bulb is fused to either an aluminum or a brass base. Aluminum bases are less expensive, but brass adheres better and makes the bulbs last longer. Bulbs also last longer in fixtures in which the bulb is positioned glass up, socket down. When bulbs hang glass side down, heat rises over the socket and shortens life.

BULB FINISHES

Decorative light bulbs come in three finishes: clear, frosted, and white.

A **clear** light bulb sparkles when it's

These three torpedo-shaped bulbs show the three finishes: clear, frosted, and white.

turned on—you can see the filament as an incandescent outline. It's this sparkle you need to lamp a fixture that is also shiny or sparkly—those made of glass, for instance, or trimmed with crystal pendants and chains of crystal beads. Clear bulbs are also a good choice for shiny chrome or highly polished brass chandeliers and sconces.

You'll also find some decorative bulbs in clear, transparent colors. These are used mostly for special effects—for holiday decorations or lamping a chandelier painted in assorted colors, such as those made of metal flowers.

Frosted bulbs have a satin finish inside the glass, which obscures the filament. When lighted, this bulb does have a hot spot in the center, where the filament is glowing, but the over-all effect is soft and diffused. Its satiny look goes well with brushed fixtures, with ceramic chandeliers, with metal that has a pewter-like, gray finish.

You get still another effect from a bulb that has fiberglass threads applied to the outside of the bulb; they're wound horizontally around the bulb, covering it completely from top to bottom. This threaded texture elongates the hot spot to give an effect that looks amazingly like a natural flame.

White bulbs are painted inside to spread the light more evenly over the entire bulb. It throws a harsher light than the other two finishes and is therefore frequently used with fixtures that use small, individual shades for each bulb. The solid white bulb also looks well when contrasted with a jet-black wrought-iron fixture.

This chandelier is lamped with a bulb (standard-size base) that has fiberglass threads applied—horizontally—to the outside surface. This elongates the hot spot to make it look more flamelike.

BULB SHAPES

When a light source is covered with a shade or shield, it doesn't matter much what the bulb looks like, so long as you get the quality of light you want. You

145

Standard shapes for decorative bulbs: 1. torpedo, standard-size base; 2. torpedo, candelabra base; 3. spire tip; 4. turn-tip flame.

Cluster of clear bulbs (torpedo-shaped) is an appropriate choice to repeat the shiny surface of the polished-brass hanging fixture.

This painted fixture looks better with a pair of frosted bulbs; the elongated spire tips of the bulbs accentuate the height of the fixture.

shop primarily for wattage when you buy your ordinary house bulbs.

But decorative bulbs are something else. They're designed to be seen and admired. To get the best quality—and looks—in decorative bulbs, look for those that are handcrafted. The glass for each bulb is blown (by mouth), and turned and shaped by hand. You can pick out the bulbs in a display rack that are handmade: no two are exactly alike.

The **torpedo or flame-shaped bulb**—not overly long, curving rather abruptly to a point—is a favorite choice for fixtures of symmetrical design. It's also the bulb that looks good inside the chimney of a converted oil lamp or in fixtures that use hurricane shades. You'll find flame-shaped bulbs in clear, frosted, and white glass, as well as transparent colors; in 25, 40, and 60 watts with either candelabra- or standard-size bases, and 15 watts in candelabra size only.

Spire-tip bulbs are offshoots of the torpedo shape, but they're more gracefully tapered, ending in a long thin point. They look good in sleek, modern fixtures, especially where you want to accentuate height. Also in traditional fixtures that are of delicate or lightly scaled design. They come in candelabra base only, in 10, 15, 25, 40, and 60 watts, and in clear or frosted glass.

A **turn-tip flame bulb** is spire-tip shape but with the point slightly bent—like a flame caught in a draft. This is the most natural-looking of the flame shapes and can be used in almost any fixture except the most severe, straight-lined modern.

Turn-tip bulbs come in either clear or frosted finishes; also in amber, ruby, and blue colors; in 25, 40, and 60 watts for both standard and candelabra bases, plus 10 and 15 watts in candelabra base only.

Perfectly **round bulbs** have made a comeback, looking as chic as a Jean Harlow movie. The satin white ones, in 10-, 15-, and 25-watt sizes, candelabra

146

Another example of spire-tip bulbs (for this fixture, the vertical line is better than a turn-tip flame). The bulbs are large in scale—in proportion to the fixture—but with candelabra bases, screwed into reducer sockets.

Bulbs with a frosted finish are a better choice than clear for a ceramic chandelier.

base, are exactly right for outlining makeup mirrors—they're flattering to the skin. (Never use a bulb of more than 25 watts for makeup mirrors—if hair spray should hit it, it will implode.) Small round bulbs in clear glass are effective when used with chrome-and-crystal fixtures (as shown at the beginning of this chapter).

Round bulbs in larger sizes are useful wherever you might want a bare-bulb look—with hanging lamp shades, for example, and with modern fixtures that may take four or more of these large bulbs in clear or white.

The large round bulbs, all with standard bases, come in several sizes; the designations G-25, G-40, G-48 refer to the diameter of the bulb. G-48, for instance, means that if you measured the diameter

Round bulbs come in assorted sizes, from tiny makeup-mirror bulbs to bulbs 6″ in diameter.

Small complexion bulbs outline a bathroom mirror to give a soft light for makeup.

A large round bulb provides dramatic lighting under a hanging shade.

Flicker-flame bulbs come in assorted sizes: 1. turn-tip flame, standard socket; 2. turn-tip flame, candelabra socket; 3. turn-tip flame in candle-flame size; 4. torpedo flame, candelabra socket; 5. torpedo flame, standard socket.

in ⅛″ increments, there would be forty-eight of them. So 48×⅛=6″ diameter. By this calculation, then, the G-40 is 5″, the G-25 is 3″. Wattage ranges from 25 to 150.

These round bulbs come in clear glass (also in clear colors in the 25-watt size), and both inside white and outside white. The outside white has a tendency to darken with age from the heat of the bulb, especially in high wattages.

FLICKER-FLAMES

The ultimate goal—especially if your fixture is copied from a design that originally used candles—is to find a bulb that looks like a real candle flame. The flicker-flame bulb comes close. Inside this bulb there's a black, flame-shaped grid that miraculously changes to a flickering red flame when you turn on the electric current.

Wattage for this bulb is low (only 2 to 3 watts); whenever the decorative effect is more important to you than the amount of light, consider using it—for night lights, wall sconces, electrified candle sticks, or outdoor post lanterns. The flicker bulb comes in torpedo and tipped-flame shapes, in both candelabra and standard bases. A round bulb with standard base is also available.

148

Examples of flickering gas-flame bulbs range from the 6. round bulb in clear and assorted clear colors; 7. tubular gas-flame bulb in clear and colors; 8. tubular frosted bulb with flickering gas flame; 9. a round bulb.

A lantern with a flickering bulb adds a delightful accent to a bookshelf. It can also be used as a night light in a child's room.

A pair of flickering bulbs in a lantern adds a welcoming note at the front door.

SPECIALTY SHAPES

Tubular bulbs are intended for fixtures mounted over paintings, but they also come in handy when you discover you haven't much space inside a converted chimney lamp. The tubular bulb may be the one you need when you replace the bulb in your fish tank; but it's also used for outdoor porch lanterns as well as for some modern chandelier designs.

You can also get tubular bulbs that flicker—to imitate gas flames. They're a real find for lamping an old gas-burning fixture that you've converted to electric lighting. The gas shades that were used to shield the gas flame look equally effective with the flickering bulb.

Tubular bulb covered with a fiberglass mantle to simulate the old-fashioned gas lamp

149

Tubular bulb with a flickering flame that imitates a gaslight

Round bulb with a flickering flame—this bulb is red, for the Christmas season.

Chimney-shaped bulb—it's frosted to make it more visible.

There's another tubular bulb designed especially for outdoor gas-fixture conversions. This bulb is covered with a fiberglass mantle to look like the old-time street lights.

The **chimney-shaped** bulb doubles as both bulb and chimney. You'll find it in standard base only, in 5″ and 6″ lengths, frosted part-way to diffuse the glare of the filament. It's a handy bulb to have when lamping a wagon-wheel fixture or an outside post lantern.

Star-shaped bulbs may be the ones you pick for holiday decorations and for Christmas or New Year's entertaining. But these small, 7-watt bulbs are equally effective for year-around use with a modern fixture of chrome rods, such as the shooting-star design shown.

The **night light** is a peanut-sized, 7-watt bulb with a candelabra base; it fits a tiny shielded fixture that plugs into a wall outlet and saves you and your guests stubbed toes when traveling down the hall at night. It's also the bulb you'll use in the base of a Victorian parlor lamp.

A **carbon-filament** bulb is a favorite with decorators and museum directors, because it most nearly duplicates the

150

mood of candlelight (without flickering). Whereas a tungsten filament is concentrated in one spot, a carbon filament can extend the length of the bulb; it illuminates with a soft, pleasing, yellowish light. These bulbs come in clear, frosted, or frosted with yellow tip—in 10- and 30-watt sizes.

A WORD ABOUT WATTAGES

The height or diameter of the bulb has nothing to do with the amount of light it throws. Light power is expressed in watts. A 40-watt and a 60-watt bulb may be exactly the same size and shape, but the 60-watt bulb will put out more light.

Most decorative bulbs come in wattages up to 60. The logical choice would seem to be the wattage you need to achieve the total light level you think ideal. But actually, when lamping a light fixture, it's sounder economy to buy the highest-wattage bulbs you can to fit your fixture, and use a dimmer (see page 121 for how to install). A bulb dimmed below its rated light level will last longer than one burning at its maximum wattage—there's less wear on the filament. It's like a log in a fireplace—lasting longer if permitted to smolder, but burning out fast if you fan the flames.

Dimmers are marked to indicate how much wattage they can handle—a maximum of 600 watts for most. That means you could lamp a six-light fixture with 100-watt bulbs or a ten-light fixture with 60-watt bulbs. Since you will seldom use that much light, you use the dimmer to pull it down to 300 watts, or even to 100 if you are using candlelight and want just a little supplementary light.

Use a galaxy of star-shaped bulbs on the ends of chrome rods that radiate from a central ball.

When you want to simulate the look of candlelight—electrically—choose the carbon-filament bulbs. The light level is low, but romantic.

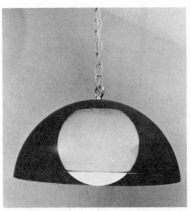

Swag a chain light over the record changer so you can see what you're doing—it hangs out of the way of the lift-up top. White chain, chosen to blend with wall, drapes to a wall hook near the ceiling and hangs down alongside the door jamb, carrying the cord to a wall outlet. Note switch set in cord at normal switch height. The plastic dome shade may be lamped with a large 100-watt round bulb. If you prefer softer, more diffused light, you can fit shade with a globe light as shown above, and use a standard 60-watt bulb. (Turn to page 154 for supplies and wiring steps for globe light.)

Another example of swag lighting suspends a handmade shade of delicately embroidered linen from a ceiling hook. (Cellophane pictured here must be removed to prevent shade from warping.) Here, the chain is slipcovered with a sheer-fabric sleeve crushed down over the chain for an elegant look. Although covered, the chain is still a necessary part of this design—to keep cord from slipping in ceiling hook and to give the shirred sleeve fullness.

CHAPTER 13

CHAIN LIGHTS

Most people don't realize how easy it is to make a chain light, or how easy it is to hang one, and so they don't appreciate what a dandy problem solver it is.

Think where you might like to use a hanging light instead of a table lamp— over a too-small bedside table, perhaps, or over the piano or record player. If your children are at an age when they might knock over table lamps, you can hang chain lights safely out of reach.

Regardless of ceiling outlets, you can situate a chain light wherever you need the light. There are three ways to do this:

1. If you have no ceiling outlet (or are using it for a chandelier), you can plug chain wiring into a wall socket, run the chain up to the ceiling, and, using ceiling hooks, place the light wherever you want it.
2. If the ceiling outlet is situated where you want your light, there's no problem. Simply cut chain the length you want, connect wiring to the ceiling outlet, and let it hang.
3. But if your ceiling outlet isn't situated where you want to drop the light—if your dining table isn't in the center of the room, for example—you can swag the chain from the outlet to the ideal location and hang the light there from a ceiling hook.

Chain wiring also permits you to regulate or change the height of the light— something that's not easy to do with table lamps or even chandeliers.

The chain itself is not only a decorative camouflage for the cord, it's necessary if you plan to swag the light. Also, if your fixture or shade is the least bit heavy, the chain carries the weight—too much drag on a cord may cause wiring to pull loose.

You'll find a wide choice of chains prepacked in kits that supply everything you need to wire and install a chain light. Chain lengths in these kits come in 3', 12', and 15' lengths. Or you can buy the chain, cord, hooks, and sockets separately. Choose from brass, copper, and chrome; shiny, brushed, antiqued, and weathered; white, black, and decorative colors; standard and heavy gauge; in loops from 5/8" to 2 1/4" long; and designs described as plain, embossed, twisted, gothic, Mediterranean, and ornate.

Cords are available in colors to blend or match with most of the chain finishes so that the cord is hardly noticeable when threaded through the chain.

SWAG LIGHT WITH A WALL PLUG

The difference between a plug-in chain light and a table lamp is mainly a difference in cord length—it takes a longer cord to swag the ceiling and reach the wall outlet. But once you've threaded cord through the chain, wired the socket, and installed two hooks in the ceiling, the light is as easy to plug in as a table lamp.

The basic supplies you will need come in prepackaged swag-light kits, or you can buy all parts separately. The socket supplied in the kit is a keyless, porcelain socket. While some chain lights can use any kind of socket, the porcelain socket is the only safe socket for lights that allow no venting for the heat of the bulb, such as enclosed glass ball shades. Porcelain sockets should also be used where glass shades hug the socket closely and when lights will be on for long periods.

Wiring the porcelain socket is only slightly different from other lamp sockets. Turn to the Glossary (page 186) to see how it's done.

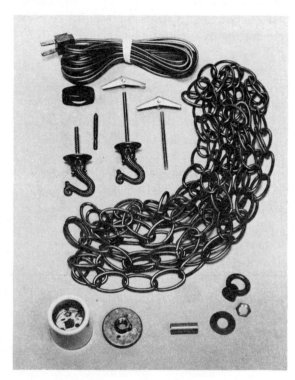

Basic supplies for a swag light

BASIC SUPPLIES:

- porcelain socket
- 1¼" nipple
- washer
- locknut
- loop
- chain, 12' or 15' depending on ceiling height
- cord with molded plug, slightly longer than chain
- 2 hooks with toggles and screws (toggles for plaster board, screws for wood)
- cord switch

For ball globe and dome shade shown, add:

- 8" neckless ball (we used plastic)
- 5¼" brass cap
- 4¾" steel insert
- 16" dome shade (we used clear-smoke plastic)

STEPS IN WIRING SWAG LIGHT:

1. Photo shows all parts strung on lamp cord. Here's the sequence: First, attach the end link of chain to loop, using chain pliers to open and close link. Thread lamp cord through chain and loop, through top of shade, through locknut, washer, top of ball cap, nipple, locknut, steel insert for ball, socket cap.
2. Wire porcelain socket and screw to cap—from inside.
3. Spin locknut onto end of nipple (this has been done in photo). Then screw nipple into socket cap—through hole in ball shade holder—to secure it.

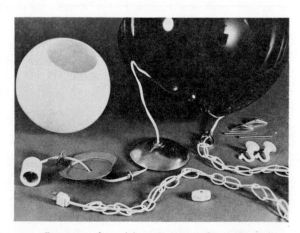

Sequence for wiring all parts of a swag light

4. Screw light bulb into socket. In this enclosed, non-ventilated ball, bulb should be no brighter than 60 watts.

5. Place plastic ball over the steel holder and bring brass cap and washer over ball; secure to nipple with locknut.

6. Guide end of nipple through inside center hole of large dome shade; pull excess wire through as you do this and secure entire assemblage by screwing loop to nipple.

7. Install first swag hook in ceiling exactly over the spot you want to light up. Use toggles or screws, depending on ceiling material.

8. Decide how much swag or drape you want across the ceiling and mark location for the second hook. You can install it in the ceiling (near the wall) or on the wall (near the ceiling). If wall is plasterboard, use the toggle. For plaster or wood, the screw will be okay—the second hook doesn't support as much weight.

9. Hang the chain on the two hooks. Slide only the chain link over the hook—not the cord.

10. Attach cord switch to lamp cord at a convenient place. **Be sure wall plug is disconnected before you do this.**

Ball of opal glass hangs by chain from an outlet over the kitchen sink. The globe opening has a neck that requires a shade holder with a 4″ fitter.

CEILING CHAIN LIGHT

If your ceiling outlet is situated where you want the light to be—directly over your dining table, for instance—and you've found a shade you'd like to hang (by chain), then all you have to do is pick up a chain ceiling-fixture kit, or equivalent supplies.

HERE'S WHAT YOU NEED

- porcelain socket
- 1¼″ nipple
- washer
- nut
- loop
- 3′ chain

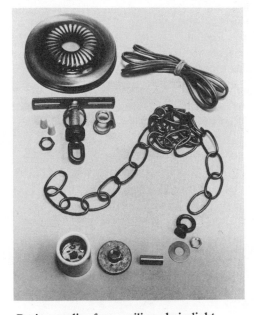

Basic supplies for a ceiling chain light

These glass shades are getting a second chance, hung singly or in clusters, suspended by chain wiring, supported by 2¼″ fitters.

In this grouping, the two center shades were originally for gaslights. The larger, "grocery store" milk-glass shade on the far right was designed for electricity and needs the 2¼″ fitter. The opalescent globe on the left takes a 3¼″ fitter; even though this fitter is vented so the heat from the bulb can escape, we recommend using a porcelain socket.

Two alternative ways to wire glass shades: with socket above or below the shade

- lamp cord for chain
- ceiling canopy
- screw-collar loop to hold up canopy
- hickey (for an old ceiling box), cross-bar (if you have a new one)
- 2 wire nuts

To wire:

1. Wire socket and attach to socket cap (see page 186).
2. Thread wire through nipple and nut. Screw nipple into socket and secure with nut.
3. Thread cord through washer, shade top (or shade fitter), and loop; then screw loop to nipple. Attach chain to loop, using chain pliers. Thread cord through chain.
4. To wire into ceiling, follow steps for Hanging the Chandelier, page 133.

CHAIN LIGHTS WITH GLASS SHADES

Small glass shades—the kind originally used on early electric chandeliers—are today's collectibles. And most of the collectors are using them for lighting, recapturing the twenties or thirties look —nostalgia for Art Deco apartments as well as old-fashioned ice-cream parlors.

The glass shades were usually in pairs or sets of four or more. Some of them survived breakage but got separated from their fixtures when houses were remodeled or torn down, so it is rare to find matching sets. Surviving gaslight shades, too, can be hung the same way, though they require 4″ fitters.

There are two ways to wire up shades that need a 2¼″ fitter, as shown at left:

1. You can hide the socket under the shade, using a dome-shaped shade holder as fitter. With this fitter, you need a socket with a pull chain—no room under the tiny shade to use a finger switch. (You can use a keyless socket if your light will be controlled by wall switch or cord switch.)

156

Wire the socket first. Screw a ½″ nipple into the socket cap, add a washer and the fitter, and secure with a locknut. Connect the chain to the loop, using chain pliers, and screw the loop onto the nipple. Thread lamp cord through loop and chain.

2. Your other choice is a socket outside —above—the shade. Choose a socket with turn-knob or push-type switch. Or use a keyless socket if controlled by a wall switch or a cord switch. Wire socket, then screw vented fitter onto the threaded, bulb end of the socket. Thread a ½″ nipple onto the cord and screw it into the socket cap; screw a locknut and loop onto the nipple. (You can omit the nipple if you use a male loop to screw into the socket cap.) Attach chain to loop using chain pliers, and thread cord through loop and chain.

To hang light, connect it to ceiling outlet following steps for Hanging the Chandelier, page 133. Or hang it as a swag light; follow directions on page 155.

SWAG LIGHTING FROM CEILING OUTLET

Center light fixtures are almost as easy to move as furniture—with the help of chain-swag lighting supplies. Should you decide to move your dining table from the center of the room to a spot closer to the window, for instance, you can move the overhead light with a length of chain and a couple of ceiling hooks. All you need for this change-over are:

- ceiling-fixture chain kit or equivalent supplies, shown on page 155
- extra lengths of matching chain—they come packaged in three-foot lengths
- new lamp cord, about a foot longer than chain. If the new location for your light is more than 4′ away from ceiling outlet, you will need an extra hook—for two swags across the ceiling.

The Tiffany-type shade used over the bedside chest (above) hangs from an antiqued-brass chain, with a ceiling canopy finished to match. The shade is the same one used for the lamp shown on page 117. As a hanging lamp, it's wired with a neckless globe to give a soft light.

To wire: Follow steps for wiring globe and dome shade on page 154. For connecting to ceiling outlet, follow Steps 1 to 4 on page 134.

Lights in a plant window keep plants healthy and at the same time add drama to the display. These lights are arranged at various levels—according to locations and heights of the plants. Each light is suspended by chain, so it can be lowered or raised as the plant grows or as new plants are brought in. For uniformity, all chain is white. Pots hang from small-size chain of same design as swag-light chain. Special plant lights are preferred as they are reflectorized, to reflect light downward and conduct heat upward. You can buy these plant light bulbs in 75- and 150-watt sizes in most plant or garden shops and in some places where regular light bulbs are sold.

CHAPTER 14

LIGHTING YOUR PLANTS

Some plants require long hours of sunlight, others thrive in shade—but all plants need light to survive and grow. If your houseplants are not getting enough light (measured in hours as well as intensity), there is something you can do about it: hang up some plant lights.

Most plants indoors need more light than comes through the windows—especially north windows. And you can easily supply it by equipping your window with plant lights. During a long siege of dreary days, or in winter, when daylight time is short, plant lights serve as an auxiliary sun.

Reflectorized bulbs used in plant lighting burn cooler than regular household bulbs of the same wattage; the built-in reflector spreads light uniformly over a larger area. Not only will these lights help you maintain the health of plants in a low-light environment but at night they bring the window to life with dramatic highlights and shadow patterns.*

Here are some of the ways you can introduce light into a plant setting:

- If you hang reflector bulbs over your plants on chain lights, you can easily raise the light to keep up with the growth of the plant—or lower it again over a young, new plant.

* Incandescent plant lights (which are rich in red light) are effective as supplementary light where your plants also get some daylight. They will help you maintain healthy plants. But if you want to grow plants, from seeds, under artificial light (little or no natural light), a mixture of incandescent light (rich in red) and fluorescent (rich in blue) light gives better results than using either one alone, according to experiments by the USDA and university horticultural departments.

- Some fixtures are designed with plant trays suspended below the light source, which makes it easy to rotate plants according to their need for extra light.
- You may want to light a tall plant from the bottom as well as overhead—such lighting casts interesting shadow patterns on ceiling or walls, too. We show how to wire flowerpots with plant lights to get up lighting. It's an especially dramatic way to light a plant in a dark corner of the room.
- Arranging plants at various heights in a window gives them more breathing room and provides more opportunity for you to create dramatic light patterns by hanging lights at varying heights.
- If you fill a plant window with a large variety of pots and plants, they'll look

Bulb wired into a clay pot can be set into any container—you see it in the lower left corner of the plant window, used as an up light in a basket. Basket is not damaged—you can tease a lamp cord through woven splints.

To wire: Wire up a ceramic socket (see Glossary, page 187). Screw short nipple into socket cap, and add locknut and washer. Slip nipple through bottom hole of pot and secure with a palnut (or any kind of locknut). Add a cord switch.

Chain light is pulled down close to a group of small plants needing extra light to maintain them. In this window, plants sit on a layer of crushed rock in a metal tray. Rocks are kept wet to maintain proper humidity in combination with lights.

Plant lights plugged into special channel

One of the clay flowerpot lights is wired to hang as a chain light; it drops from ceiling hook, swagged from ceiling outlet or wall socket. To wire, follow directions for basket light on previous page, but substitute a loop for the palnut and attach the length of chain you need.

tidier if you hang them all from chains suspended from ceiling hooks—the same chain you use for the swag or chain lighting. This is a good way to use leftover chain from lighting installations.

• Photo shows another way to hang plants—from a bracket-mounted clothes pole. As plants grow and change in shape, you can move them easily to any spot along the pole.

• When you add auxiliary lighting for plants, remember that it has a drying effect—your plant window will require some means of stepping up humidity. The evaporation of water from pebble-filled plant trays, along with daily misting, will do wonders for your plants.

By attaching a Tap-a-line channel to the top of your window, you can plug in a series of plant lights without special wiring. Simply push in plug prongs anywhere along the channel. Tap-a-line comes in 1′, 2′, 3′, and 6′ lengths and plugs into any wall outlet.

Lighting for plants on a porch or enclosed patio

Brackets used at this plant window (see photo, opposite page) have expandable hooks; they extend from 8″ to 12″ and can be adjusted to accommodate the changing diameter of plants. Brackets also support an aluminum rod from which to hang additional plants and lights. By installing ceiling hooks in front of the rod, you could hang more plants; look for swivel hooks so you can rotate plants for even growth. Use leftover chain for hanging an accent piece, such as the crystal balls shown here—rescued from a discarded chandelier.

Plants at various heights, in a variety of natural-looking containers (baskets, clay pots, terra-cotta flue liners), and sparked with lights and interesting accessories, make an effective arrangement on a porch or enclosed patio (see photo, opposite page). The plant lights are all wired into clay flowerpots (see details below). Old gas-plate and wagon-wheel hub both serve as plant risers (or the wagon-wheel hub can be wired to make an unusual lamp base, see page 166).

If you unearth a carved newel-post finial at some flea market, you can turn it into a hanging plant holder. Use leftover chain or buy a couple packages of three-foot lengths from your local store. Attach chain to each corner of the base with a sturdy screw eye.

Another wired flowerpot was placed inside one of the flue liners, where it serves as an up light, casting a spider-plant shadow onto the ceiling. Other potted lights sit on the floor behind both the large and small schefflera plants.

Clay is heatproof; you can safely rest the clay-pot light on its side, to light plants at floor level. Here, the piggyback plant gets a light boost.

Wrought-iron lamp bracket with swing arm doubles as a distinctive plant holder. Or, if it's in a location where you can use an up light, replace the plant with a wired flowerpot.

Here are some flea-market finds with possibilities for a second life as useful lamps. Nothing in this assortment of junk cost more than $5. You can see most of these items, restored and rewired, in Chapter 15. Look for the two brown bottles in Chapter 3, the Art Deco base in Chapter 9, the brass wall sconce in Chapter 10, and the milk-glass shade in Chapter 13.

FLEA-MARKET FINDS MADE INTO LAMPS

Prowling flea markets is the great American pastime—the lure of finding a real treasure for pennies. Nostalgia for "the good old days" provides some of the incentive. But your forays will be more fun—and more productive—when you train your eyes to look for shapes and forms among the discards. Root through boxes of old hardware; inspect odds and ends of machine parts or a tangle of sconces and chandeliers salvaged from demolished buildings; keep a sharp eye peeled for wood turnings. Under the tables—that's where you'll find the buys for "pennies."

Many of these never-meant-to-be lamp bases will make the most interesting lamp designs of all. Pictures in this chapter will inspire you: the wagon-wheel hub that makes a rustic lamp base, the balustrade post that becomes a table lamp, the finial turned upside down to hang as a wall sconce, the glass chimney filled with flowers to hide the lamp pipe.

Learn to look twice at the trashy or poorly designed lamp that often turns up in thrift shops. Imagine how you might pull it apart and remake it into a more pleasing design.

You'll be able to convert some of your finds into lamps elegant enough for living room or bedroom. Others will be better suited to rooms in vacation homes or other less formal rooms. And some will be just for fun—a crazy kind of light for your tool shop or potting shed.

Starting with someone else's junk, you can design and wire lamps, often with no more equipment than might be found in

Three rusty wheel hubs lying in the grass at an outdoor flea market hardly looked like a lamp base—until we mentally stacked them. To build height for this "openwork" lamp, we assembled it on a stock wood base 4½″ in diameter. From ¾″ lumber, we cut three wood disks, 4½″ in diameter, drilling them for lamp pipe and sandwiching them between the 4¼″ metal rings. The third disk, on top, is covered with a 2¾″ brass cap. Painted a rich chocolate brown, the wood additions blend with the rusty color of metal after it was cleaned and rubbed with lemon oil. See Chapter 1 for wiring directions.

We decided to leave the brass-finished threaded lamp pipe as is—to blend with the brushed-brass shade. For a dressier lamp, we would have slipcovered the threaded pipe with plain brass tubing. Height of lamp, 25″.

Clear-glass chimney from an old lamp makes an ideal showcase for a floral design, which, in turn, will hide lamp pipe. You'll need a stock wood base to fit the 4″ bottom opening; use Rub 'n' Buff to give it a brass finish to match the 3″ brass cap which will be clamped over the top of the chimney when you tighten up the assembly. Insert lamp pipe in wood base, with washer and hex nut to hold it in place.

To make the dried-flower arrangement (before you wire up the lamp), cover exposed length of lamp pipe with plastic foam this way: Whittle grooves in two long pieces of foam and snug them around the pipe, holding them together with florist's wire. Trim plastic to form a column about 1½″ in diameter. Poke stems of dried flowers into foam until it is completely covered; be sure flower column is no more than 4″ in diameter, so you can slip the chimney over it. Clamp the brass cap in place at top with a locknut, and add harp wings and socket cap. Wire, following directions in Chapter 1. Total lamp height, 22″.

Wood turnings make attractive lamp bases for vinyl or parchment shades, too. This one in a natural finish emphasizes the grain of the wood —most attractive with the white pleated vinyl shade. Drilling a hole through the center of a big table leg is no project for a home shop, however. It's easier to saw the leg in half lengthwise, gouge out a center channel in each half for the rod, and clamp it back together again with glue. Attach a square lamp base and wire as in Chapter 1.

Two finds add up to one unusual table lamp— the cased-glass dome shade is supported by an old balustrade post (or you might find an old table leg that would serve). This post was 18″ long with a 3″ cube at one end; to give the proposed lamp a steadier base (and better proportions, too), we attached a second base 5½″ square, 1½″ deep. At the top, precisely in the center, we drilled a ⅜″ hole 1″ deep and screwed in a 1½″ nipple. We slipped a flat brass cap over the nipple and added a 14″ ring shade holder for the 14″ antique dome shade. For light, we wired a socket with a side hole and screwed that onto the nipple. The lamp cord is glued into one of the grooves in the post; with that side to the wall, you never see it. Over-all height, 30″.

an apartment toolbox. On these pages, we show an assortment of "for instances." Only a few require more sophisticated tools; a saw and clamps for cutting and gluing special-size bases; a power drill, a miter box, etc. If you don't have a basement workbench, cultivate a friend who does!

If you are in doubt as to the best or easiest way to turn your discoveries into usable lamps, look back through the preceding fourteen chapters. The step-by-step photos show you how to cope with every kind of wiring you may encounter.

And you'll find it's exhilarating, working with your hands and brain in this creative way: solving problems, turning **nothing** into **something.** A few triumphs and you could become addicted, with a new hobby to pursue. It's possible you'll generate such a demand for your designs, from friends and friends of friends, that you may even find yourself in a bright new business.

Metal strainer from an old cream separator is an ideal shape and size for a chain-hung shade in a country kitchen. The strainer, 12″ in diameter, 8″ deep, easily accommodates a porcelain socket and 5″ round bulb; for wiring instructions, see chain lights, page 155. Unexpected bonus: the light reflected through holes of strainer spreads a rosette pattern on the ceiling.

Sometimes you will find a bargain lamp in a thrift shop; take a minute for inspection and see if minor design changes will save it. This candlestick lamp was 49″ tall—almost junior-floor-lamp size—much too tall for the usual-height end table. We shortened the lamp from both ends. We removed the iron scroll base, substituting an eight-sided stock wood base which was finished to blend with the candlestick. At the top, the candle spacer was replaced with a check ring and neck. The old shade, 20″ deep, was replaced with one only 14″ deep. Over-all height of the *new* lamp is now 34″ —much better for end-of-sofa reading.

Old wagon-wheel hub makes a fascinating lamp base. To hold lamp pipe securely through center of hub, fasten a 6″ crossbar (center hole tapped for lamp pipe) across the bottom opening. Fasten lamp pipe to crossbar with locknut. At top of lamp, slip a 6″ cap over the pipe and hub; add a 2″ spacer (with check rings to fit top and bottom of spacer) and secure with locknut. Drill a hole in the side of the metal ring band at bottom of lamp; thread lamp cord through hole and up lamp pipe. Add harp wings and wire socket, following directions in Chapter 1, Steps 9–14. Over-all height, 28″.

Wire an ordinary canning-jar lid and you can turn any fruit jar—quart or half-gallon size—into an amusing kitchen lamp. Fill the jar with anything you want to display: lentils, macaroni, rocks, shells, even a terrarium!

Wire a socket with a side hole. Spin a short neck onto nipple and screw top of nipple into socket cap. Bore a ⅜″ hole in the center of jar lid. Spin bottom of nipple through hole in lid; add a large washer (same diameter as lid is best) and secure with locknut. Set lid and socket over jar opening and tighten the lid. Add bulb and clip-on shade. Total height of quart-jar lamp is 14″.

To guide midnight snackers to the kitchen, make a pin-up night light by mounting a grater on an old wooden slaw cutter. A flat bracket attaches candelabra socket to the wood back. You can use either a rotary switch (see how-to instructions in Glossary) or use a cord switch (see page 59).

166

A tin cracker box is easy to wire and what more appropriate lamp base could you find for a kitchen shelf? Lamp is 22" high over all; the can is 9" high, 4½" square; shade 12" in diameter. Second photo shows what you need for the wiring job. Secure 13¼" lamp pipe to bottom of 5" wood base with washer and locknut. Drill a 7/16" hole in center of both top and bottom of can and slip can over lamp pipe. At top, add 3¾" cap, then a 2"×⅞" spacer with two ⅞" check rings at top and bottom of spacer; secure all with locknut. Thread lamp cord into side hole of base and up the pipe; add harp wings and wire socket following directions in Chapter 1, Steps 9–14. Paint the base, cap, and spacer to match printing on tin box.

Here's a light spoof for the potting shed or workshop—and a good, sturdy lamp besides! Base is an old blow torch bored for lamp pipe. The 6" length of exposed pipe is covered with copper tubing. Inside the colander shade, you need a clip-on shade adapter (see page 37), which goes through the center hole and is locked in with a finial. Over-all height, 19½".

A wide or bulky lamp base will provide better light if you wire it with more than one socket. This antique demijohn, handblown deep green glass, 20″ high, is equipped with a two-light cluster fitted securely into the bottle neck with rubber adapters (see Chapter 3). The burlap shade is oval to go with the oval bottle shape. Over-all height, 30″.

Turn an old oak finial upside down—your discerning eye may envision a wall sconce. All you need is to figure out how to hang it. This 12″ finial hangs by a metal strap, bent at a right angle and set flush into a sconce top.

To wire: Bore a ⅜″ hole, 1″ deep, in the center of sconce top and screw in a 2¼″ nipple. Slip a flat brass cap (4¼″ in diameter to cover the top) over the exposed end of nipple, cupped side up. Wire a candelabra socket (adjustable to 4¾″) to the nipple (see page 56), and cover with a 6″ candle cover (socket plus exposed nipple equals 6″). Finish top with a 4″ ball shade holder with gallery—glue this to brass cap. Cord exits through hole in metal strap and down wall to outlet.

Ten-sided Mexican tin vase has a graceful urn shape, ideal for lamp base. Since it is most unlikely ever to have antique value, we drilled a hole in the bottom and (with the lamp pipe) attached the vase to a wood base 2¼″ high; vase itself is only 11½″ high. Urn is antiqued in blue, base is painted charcoal gray to simulate cut stone, and the cap is painted to match. Cone-shaped shade is also charcoal with white lining, 18″ in diameter. Over-all height, 26″.

ILLUSTRATED GLOSSARY

You don't need to know electrician's lingo to order the parts you need for wiring a lamp or fixture. If you tell your electrical-supply dealer what you want to use the parts for, he will know what to give you.

But as you delve more into creative lamp making and restoration, you'll be looking for alternative, innovative, or unorthodox solutions to some of your more challenging projects. It will help you immensely to know what else is available—and how to ask for it.

THREAD SIZES

Screwing parts together is what lamp assembly is all about. Thus, thread-size terminology is basic to so many of the specifications and definitions in this book, we're putting it here, at the head of the Glossary, for your ready reference.

Threaded pipe and nipples come in different sizes. Some (but not all) are described with the electrician's code letters IP. At one time, IP was an abbreviation for iron pipe. Today, its meaning is defined by the fraction used with it . . . and (unfortunately for logical minds) this fraction is not a description of the actual size as measured by a schoolboy's ruler. So. . . .

- ⅛-IP designates a threaded pipe or nipple that has an outside diameter (O.D.) of ⅜″. The thread size is that which fits the ordinary lamp socket. Thus, ⅛-IP is the thread and pipe size used for assembling table lamps.

- ¼-IP designates a threaded pipe or nipple with an O.D. of ½″. This is the thread size you need for the pipe in floor lamps, and the thread size for nipples you may need when installing ceiling fixtures.

THREAD SIZES – (SHOWN FULL SIZE)

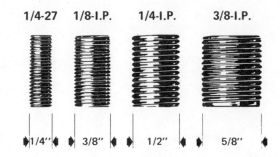

1/4-27   1/8-I.P.   1/4-I.P.   3/8-I.P.

1/4″   3/8″   1/2″   5/8″

- ⅜-IP designates a threaded pipe or nipple with an O.D. of ⅝″. This is the size of stud threads in the old-fashioned ceiling outlets; also the size of gas-pipe outlets.

When IP is not part of the thread size, then you know the size is being stated in ordinary fractions. For example:

- ¼-27 means a thread that is of ¼″ outside diameter, 27 threads to the inch. This size thread is used on top of harps, so most finials are tapped ¼-27 (some finials are also available tapped ⅛-IP). Though ¼-27 sounds larger than ⅛-IP, it's actually smaller.
- ⁷⁄₁₆″ is the size of the opening in caps, canopies, and lamp bases that are designed to slip over ⅛-IP pipe. So if you ever need to drill a pipe hole for a lamp you're designing, choose the ⁷⁄₁₆″ drill bit.

F and M refer to female and male threading. A loop labeled ⅛-IP-F means that the loop will screw *onto* a ⅛-IP pipe or nipple. One labeled ⅛-IP-M means that the loop threads screw *into* a ⅛-IP coupling—or *into* a crossbar tapped ⅛-IP.

Tapped refers to screw threads on an inside surface; threaded refers to threads on the outside surface.

BASES for lamps

A base can add the necessary finishing touch to a lamp and provide a side hole for the lamp cord. When necessary, a base can also add stability, either by weight or size (or both), to keep the lamp from tipping.

You can buy bases made of metal—brass or plated; in plain, fancy-filagree, or molded designs. Or carved teak—Chinese style and usually painted black. Marble squares are available in various sizes (with sides straight up and down) so you can stack two of them for a graduated base.

The largest selection of shapes and sizes are available in wood. Square, cut-corner square, hexagonal, octagonal, round. Round bases come flat-topped or with rim. Choose flat-tops

about ¼″ larger than lamp bottom all around; rimmed tops should fit lamp vase or column exactly.

All bases (except marble) flare out to a larger size at the bottom. Metal bases are hollow; wood bases have a recessed hole deep enough to accommodate the lamp pipe secured with washer and nut. Wood bases are bored with side hole for cord exit.

You can also buy figurine bases in both wood and metal—the hole for lamp pipe is drilled off center to free center of base for the art object.

BUSHINGS for reducing holes

When you want to reduce the size of a hole, you need to know about these brass fittings. There's one for almost any job that will come up. For example:

- a headless brass reducing bushing, ⅜-M✕⅛-F can reduce the large opening in a gas sconce to a size that can be screwed onto regular ⅛-IP (see page 127).
- a ⅛-F✕¼-M nozzle screwed onto a ⅛-IP pipe or fixture socket makes it possible to add a shade and finial (see page 67).
- a cord inlet bushing reduces a hole to lamp-cord size and gives a smooth finish to the hole, helping to eliminate abrasion of the cord. You'd use this in the side opening (tapped ⅛-IP) of a coupling with a side hole (see page 59).

No matter what problem you have, there's likely to be a reducer to solve it. Ask your dealer for his suggestions.

CANOPIES

Canopy is the name for the cover that hides wires and outlet in the ceiling. There are various kinds, because there are various ways to mount them.

- **Canopy with 1¹⁄₁₆″ center hole.** Easy to put up with a screw-collar loop: with canopy in

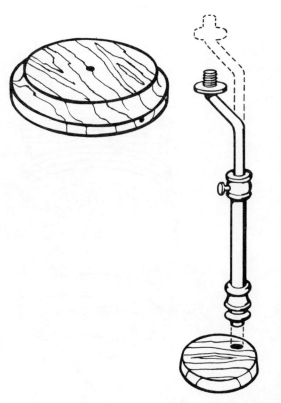

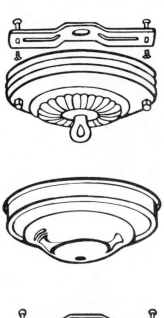

place, spin loop onto outlet nipple; push canopy snug against ceiling; and secure with collar.

• **Canopy with ⅞₁₆″ center hole** may have two mounting holes bored near edge. A plain loop in the center holds the fixture, while the canopy is snugged against the ceiling with two long screws into the crossbar.

• **Canopy with ⅞₁₆″ center hole and no mounting holes** is held to the ceiling by regular loop. Here's how to make it snug: Mount crossbar onto lugs of square ceiling box, and screw a 1¾″ nipple (tapped ⅛-IP) into center hole. Slip canopy over nipple, and screw regular loop threaded ⅛-IP onto nipple. Adjust placement of canopy by raising and lowering nipple, then lock nipple in place with locknut.

• **Canopy with convenience outlet.** This canopy has a hook in the center on which to hang the fixture and an electric outlet beside the hook, into which you plug the fixture. The advantage of this canopy is that it's very easy to take down a chandelier when you want to clean or polish the crystals.

• **Flush-type outlet concealer.** When you want to remove a fixture and close up the ceiling temporarily or permanently, cover it with an outlet concealer. First, tape up exposed ends of the lead wires, separately. Feed them through the ⅝″ hickey attached to the concealer, and spread them out of the way. Screw hickey onto the stud protruding from outlet box. Keep spinning it on until the plate is flush against the ceiling. If stud isn't long enough, get a **ceiling outlet extension** (1″ long) to extend the stud downward. If one isn't enough, use two.

CAPS

Most lamp bodies need a topping—to cover up a hole, as for a vase lamp; or to make a graceful curve between a flat-top body and neck. Ask for a vase cap. It's made of brass, unfinished or brushed and lacquered; sizes

174

range from 1½" to 7" in diameter, in ⅛" gradations.

Sometimes you may prefer a brass plate (as for the balustrade lamp in Chapter 15). It's cupped, like a large check ring; size range is 2" to 6" in diameter, in ¼" gradations.

CHAIN and chain accessories

Chain is as useful as it is ornamental. Strong enough to support heavy fixtures, indestructible for hanging plants, it also drapes gracefully for swag lights. It's available in a wide choice of decorative patterns and many link shapes and sizes, in bright or antique finishes as well as decorator colors. It is sold in 3' packages, or—in some shops—by the foot from a reel.

Swag hooks for chains match the chains in color and finish; they're packaged with toggle bolts (for installation on plasterboard ceilings) and screws (for wood joists). Select the type you need.

Swivel hooks make a 360° turn; that means hanging plants can be rotated to take advantage of sunlight or turned "best face" into the room whenever you wish. In clear plastic, they blend into ceiling, whatever color it is.

Chain pliers make light work of opening and closing chain links. The nose spreads the link; notches between handles close the links without kinking the shape or marring the finish.

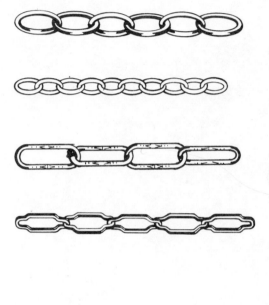

CHECK RINGS

They are often used as caps, or to center the pipe in lamp bases that have a large top opening. They come in sizes ranging from ½" to 2", all with a ⁷⁄₁₆" center hole, which slips over ⅛-IP lamp pipe.

Brass check rings are also used under candle cups or candle-socket covers and on both top and bottom of spacers.

CORD for lamp and fixtures

A **standard lamp cord** contains two plastic-sheathed wires; it's called No. 18/2, meaning it has two wires No. 18 size. The wire is not solid wire, however; it's many hair-fine copper wires, so the cord will be flexible and supple.

The plastic covering is an improvement over rubber, which used to dry out and crack with age. Also, there's a wider range of cord colors to choose from in plastic. Besides the usual white, brown, and black, you'll find opaque gold, transparent gold, and transparent silver (clear).

White is a good choice when you have a white china or porcelain base, but it tends to soil easily and is difficult to clean. Brown is the staple for wood or wood-base lamps, dark glass or pottery, copper; black for wrought-iron bases or tin lanterns.

Opaque gold is a good neutral tone that you look for when you need an unobtrusive color —for pottery lamps or chain-swags, for instance. Perhaps the most versatile of all is the transparent gold—just right for brass candlesticks, brass-trimmed bases, brass fixtures, brass chains. Transparent silver blends well with crystal, pewter, silver, clear glass.

Most lamp cords are sold with plugs molded to the cord. This plug is practically indestructible and it saves you the bother of shopping for and installing your own. Standard lengths for these plugged cords are 6', 8', and 10' for lamps; 15' and 20' for swag lights —for all colors except transparent silver, which you buy from spools, by the foot.

Fixture wire is a single strand of No. 18 wire.

COUPLINGS

Couplings with ⅛-IP female threads are used to join two pieces of standard lamp pipe or nipples. Some couplings have a side hole, handy for side exit of lamp cord. If the coupling shows, finish off the side hole with a cord-inlet bushing.

FINIALS

Finials not only lock the shade to the harp, they also add the "crowning" decorative touch to the lamp. Those of brass are most available, in many sizes, shapes, and designs—from simple turnings to eagles, acorns, balls, pineapples. For more elaborate lamps, you can also find finials of delicate filigrees, precious and semiprecious stones, crystal. Worth looking for if you have a fine Chinese urn or a valuable crystal vase you're converting into a lamp.

HARPS

There are two types of harps used for most lamps: screw-on and detachable.

The screw-on harp is a real time saver when you want to convert a lamp with a clip-on shade to one with a regular shade and finial. You simply screw the harp onto the top of the socket—that's all there's to it! This harp automatically positions a shade 2″ higher (that's the height of the socket) than the harp size indicates. That means a 7″ harp will actually take a shade 9″ deep; a 9″ harp will have a clearance of 11″.

The detachable harp consists of two pieces: the harp wing, which fits over the lamp pipe and is held in place by the socket, and the harp itself, which locks into the wing with two small metal sleeves. It's the most popular harp for table lamps, because (1) you can pack the lamp into a compact carton (for shipping or for storing) when you remove the protruding harp top, and (2) it's so simple to switch harps when trying on lamp shades to get the correct height for the shade of your choice—no need to take the whole lamp apart. Though a 10″ harp is the most popular, you can choose from sizes ranging from 7″ to 13″ (in ½″ gradations), so there's sure to be a right size for any shade.

Both types of harps are topped with shade holders that swivel—makes it easy to keep

shades straight. The swivel has a threaded stud (¼-27), onto which you screw the finial.

HICKEY

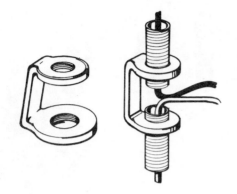

Hickey is a U-shaped connection usually used in old ceiling installations to join stud (which is ⅜-IP) and nipple (⅛-IP); such a hickey would be labeled ⅛ × ⅜. Hickeys are also available tapped with same-size threading (⅛ × ⅛) to interrupt lamp-pipe joining for side exit of wires, as shown in sketch.

KITS

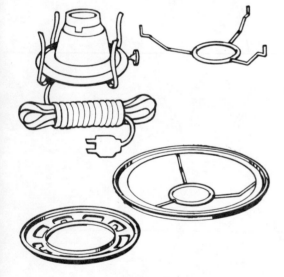
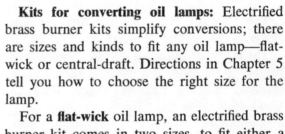

Kits for converting oil lamps: Electrified brass burner kits simplify conversions; there are sizes and kinds to fit any oil lamp—flat-wick or central-draft. Directions in Chapter 5 tell you how to choose the right size for the lamp.

For a **flat-wick** oil lamp, an electrified brass burner kit comes in two sizes, to fit either a No. 1 or No. 2 opening, 2⅝" or 3" chimney. Chimney is held by four prongs. Burner may also be fitted with a tripod or a ring holder for 7" or 10" glass shade—or with a 4" ring to hold a ball shade.

You can also buy these kits wired for **two-way** (up-and-down) lights—turn on both lights at once, or each one separately. (See page 90.)

For a **round-wick,** central-draft lamp, the electrified brass burner is sized to fit specific brand-name lamps, or by diameter of the neck. For instance, Rayo takes a 2¼" threaded bottom; Rochester, 2⅜". This converter also has four prongs to hold chimney and can be fitted with 10" rings or tripods for glass shades.

Another-style oil-lamp converter uses a **neck adapter.** Choose a No. 1, No. 2, or No.

178

3 brass adapter to fit your lamp font or neck (see page 77). Socket housing, attached to adapter with nipple and locknut, is also a brass-plated chimney holder—with a gallery instead of prongs. Chimney holder has side exits for lamp cord and turn knob. You can also get ring, tripod, or ball-shade holders to fit around the chimney-holder gallery.

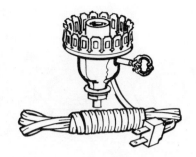

Kits for bottle lamps: See Chapter 3.

Kits for canopy-hung fixtures: See Chapter 11.

Kits for chain lights: See Chapter 13.

Kits for platform lamps: See Chapter 7.

Kits for rewiring lamps: See Chapter 1.

Kits for vase lamps: See Chapter 6.

LOADERS

Loaders add weight to a lamp base to keep the lamp from toppling over too easily. Place a loader in the cavity of a metal base, or inside the body of the lamp if you use a wood base. Loaders come in 2½″ to 5″ diameters; ½ to 2½ pounds in weight. They have a 7/16″ center hole that slips over the pipe and a grooved wireway for side exit of lamp cord.

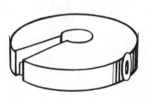

LOCKNUTS

Locknuts are thin nuts available in steel and brass, in thread sizes to fit all standard pipe and nipple sizes; they're essential to screw down a lamp assembly and hold it tight.

Knurled brass locknuts are used on any visible part of the lamp; for example, at the top of the lamp, before you screw socket to lamp pipe. Depend on the locknut to hold all the lamp parts together—never ask a socket to do this job.

The round, flat locknut also serves to fill in the space between the lamp pipe and the center hole in the cap. Edge is knurled so you can

179

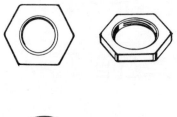

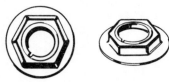

get a good finger grip on it to tighten it. If you use pliers, take care not to strip the edge—some craftsmen pad their pliers.

Hexagonal locknuts are used where they don't show, as at the base of a lamp. Their shape makes tightening easier because you can get a good grip on them with pliers, wrench, or hex-key. Hex nuts are also available in brass.

Palnuts are a combination of hex nut and washer, often doing the job of both. They're molded in tough steel, usually used only in places where they don't show. Also available brass-plated.

LOOPS

Loops are essential for installing ceiling canopies and for hanging chain lights—the chain attaches to the loop. In addition, the loop has a passageway for lamp cord that threads from socket to ceiling outlet. Loops come with male or female threading, ⅛-IP in diameters of ¾", ¹⁵⁄₁₆", and 1½".

For a screw-collar loop threaded ¼-IP and used for canopies with a 1¹⁄₁₆" hole, see page 134.

NECKS AND SPINDLES

Brass necks provide a graceful transition between body of lamp and socket. Sizes range from ⅝" to 1⁵⁄₁₆" high; tall lamps may need a spindle instead of or in addition to a neck, or a combination of two necks. You can buy necks completely threaded (tapped ⅛-IP) to screw onto lamp pipe. Or with a smooth ⁷⁄₁₆" hole that slips over lamp pipe—in which case you would need to fasten the neck down with a locknut.

Brass spindles are like necks, except they're taller, up to 4½", and there's more choice of design in turnings.

Both necks and spindles are also available in brass-finish plastic. Lighter in weight than solid brass, plastic necks are often used for inexpensive lamps. Check when you buy, to make sure you're getting what you want.

NIPPLES

Nipples are short pieces of threaded pipe. You'll need assorted lengths—to add a few inches when your lamp pipe comes up short. Use a coupling if the connection will be hidden inside the lamp (figure a). At the top of a lamp, a neck will serve as coupling (figure b). You'll need nipples for converting bottles and candlesticks into lamps. Also when installing ceiling fixtures and wall sconces—in both ⅛-IP and ¼-IP sizes.

You can buy nipples in assorted sizes and lengths wherever lamp pipe is sold—in steel or brass-plated. Or make your own nipples by sawing lengths from threaded pipe.

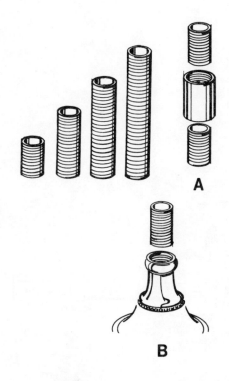

A

B

PIPE for lamps

Lamp pipe is the backbone of any lamp design—it holds all the parts together. This pipe has an outside diameter (O.D.) of ⅜″, but what you ask for is ⅛-IP. See explanation under Thread Sizes, at the beginning of Glossary.

You can buy 4″, 6″, 8″, 10″, and 12″ lengths of pipe, threaded at both ends. But unless you know the exact length you need, you make a smarter buy if you get pipe threaded the entire length. Then you can cut it to the exact length you need and it will always be threaded at each end, no matter where you cut it. There's no waste—even the shortest leftover pieces can be used as nipples.

Use a hacksaw to cut threaded pipe. For professional results, spin two hex nuts onto the pipe—one on each side of the cut line. (See page 28.) After the rod is sawed, slowly "back out" with the nuts. They'll clear out any burrs caused by the sawing.

You can buy lamp pipe in steel or brass-plated.

BRASS TUBING

There are times when you want to cover up the threaded pipe—as for a clear-glass lamp base. For this you can buy plain brass tubing; you need ¼-IP tubing (½″ O.D.) to slip over the threaded ⅛-IP pipe. It's available also in steel, and in unfinished, brushed-and-lacquered, and polished-and-lacquered brass.

PLUGS

If for some reason you need to replace a plug, you have several quick-to-wire plugs to choose from:

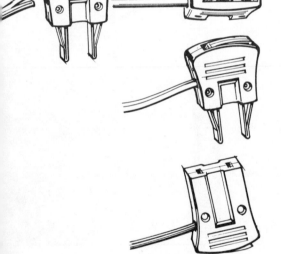

Plug with a lift-up lever: To wire, split the insulation between wire ends for about ¼″; lift lever of plug into vertical position; push wire ends into side of plug (you'll be able to see one end slide under a small molded protrusion in plug, other end stays up); push down the lever. That's it!

NOTE: Should you want to make an extension cord, there's a female plug for the other end of the cord; wire exactly as the male plug.

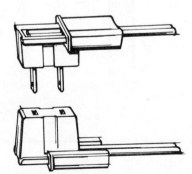

Automatic plug with slide-on top: To wire, slide the top off; lay wire ends flat, onto top of open plug (don't pull wires apart this time)—there are two small prongs to pierce the wires to make contact; slide top back on.

This plug also has a matching female plug for making up an extension cord.

End-loading automatic plug: To wire, pull out center mechanism; insert wire through hole in outer cover and push into hole of center part; push wired center back into cover.

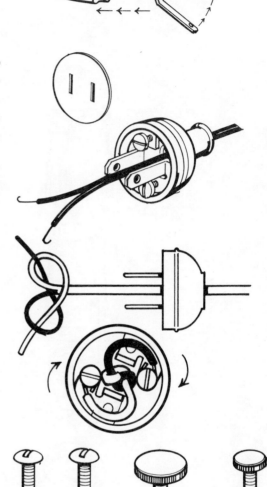

Standard plastic or rubber plug: As in lamp sockets, these plugs have two exposed terminal screws. Wire them as you would a socket: pull the two wires apart, remove insulation from wire ends; twist exposed wires clockwise, hook onto screws (clockwise), and tighten.

One difference: You need to tie an underwriter's knot to relieve tension on wire ends. Diagram at right shows how. Be sure to complete the wiring by adding cardboard insulators that cover the screws.

SCREWS

Screws used for lamps and fixtures have a standard, $\frac{8}{32}$, thread size. There are round heads and knurled flat heads; short "holder" screws for holding shades in their fitters or holding ceiling shades; and long screws for mounting a canopy to a crossbar.

SHADE RISERS

Shade risers are handy when you want to "raise the shade just a trifle"—to heights that are in between harp sizes. They're also less expensive than the replacement of a harp. These risers are designed to screw onto the stud of the harp—before you add the shade and finial.

Shade risers can be used also as "finial risers" to make the finial more visible on deep shades. When used for this purpose, you slip the shade over the stud first, then add riser and finial.

SOCKETS

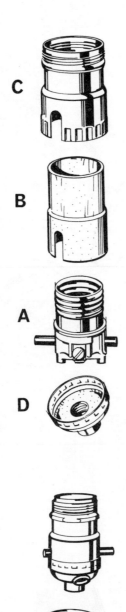

Lamp sockets are made up of four parts:

A. Inner, "working part" consists of a plastic unit that houses the intricate mechanism for lighting up a lamp with a simple turn of the switch. It has two terminal screws—one brass, one nickel—onto which the wire ends are fastened. Plus a grooved metal receptacle into which you screw the bulb.

B. Paper shell fits over this central unit and serves as insulation between the core and outside metal cover.

C. Metal cover slips over the paper shell. It's threaded on one end—for screw-on-type harps or screw-on-type bridge-lamp shades.

D. Metal cap locks onto the crimped end of cover and is threaded to fit any standard lamp rod. Some caps also have a setscrew, which keeps the socket from loosening up due to constant pulling or pushing—as with a pull chain. (It's required for any lamp with UL label.)

Turn to Chapter 1 for steps in wiring a socket.

When shopping for a socket, you can choose from several designs and switch controls: push-through, pull-chain, turn-knob, 3-way turn-knob, 3-wire turn-knob, keyless, side-hole.

Push-through sockets are designed for lamps that use one level of light—"on" and "off" only. A good choice for small lamps, converted oil lamps, boudoirs, and accent lights.

Pull-chain socket is used whenever the socket is difficult to reach—as with cluster lights when the sockets are situated near the top of the shade; for swag lights when the socket is enclosed by a glass ball or shade; for lamps with glass shades that hug the socket.

3-way turn-knob socket is almost standard these days for any new table lamp. It's such a versatile socket, because you can use it with either standard or 3-way (such as 50-100-250-watt) bulbs.

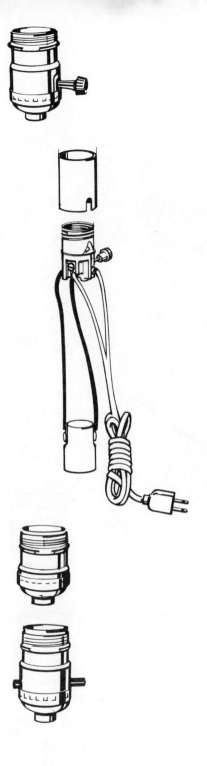

3-wire control socket makes it possible to control two bulbs, as for the up-and-down lights of the Victorian lamp on page 91. One turn of the switch lights the top globe only, another turn lights the bottom only, a third turn lights both bulbs.

Turn-knob sockets look like the 3-way but have only on-and-off control. You'll need this type for any lamp with a glass chimney. It's also the socket to choose when you wish to use a decorative key, as for a Rayo lamp. Or if you need to extend the length of the knob, as for some traditional lamps. You can, of course, use decorative keys and extensions on any turn-knob socket—on-off, 3-way, or 3-wire.

Keyless socket is the best choice for any light that is controlled by a wall switch, when you have a switch at the base of the lamp, or when it is handier to have a switch in the lamp cord.

Side-hole sockets permit the cord to exit from the side, making it possible to wire a valuable vase, candlestick, or decanter without having to drill it for lamp pipe. Side-hole sockets are usually push-through-controlled. If you want a 3-way socket with a side hole, buy both sockets and just change socket caps.

Most sockets are available in brass finish, solid brass, aluminum, molded plastic, and porcelain. More than 90 per cent of the sockets used today are of the brass-finish variety.

Solid brass is often preferred for valuable antique lamps. Also for lamps used at the seashore—salt air doesn't corrode brass as it does aluminum and steel. If you own a lamp that was made before 1940, chances are that it has a solid brass socket. In those days, brass was cheaper than aluminum.

Aluminum sockets are the least expensive —a sensible choice for any lamp in which the socket doesn't show. Or for silver or pewter bases.

Porcelain sockets are used wherever you have excessive heat or where heat from the bulb cannot escape.

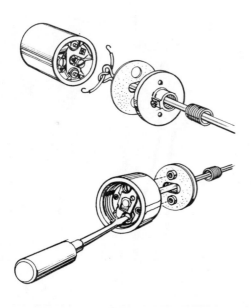

A porcelain socket has two parts: (1) porcelain socket body and (2) die-cast metal cap, which has cardboard insulation on socket side and a threaded ⅛-IP neck and setscrew. This socket is usually used with a nipple. So, when wiring, thread lamp cord through nipple first, then socket cap; split cord and knot the two wires. Strip and twist wire ends, and attach clockwise to each of socket screws (sketch a).

Fasten socket cap to porcelain body from inside socket: fit the two screw ends into holes tapped for them in cap; turn screws until you have a tight fit to lock up the socket (sketch b). Screw nipple into cap and lock it in with setscrew.

Socket extension raises the bulb upward 1″ (see page 36).

Socket adapter reduces a socket from standard to candelabra size.

UNDERCOVER SOCKETS

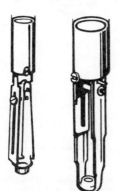

There are some sockets that don't show. Most common are those covered with imitation candles, which you see in chandeliers or converted candlestick designs. For wiring or rewiring such "candle" lamps, you need adjustable sockets. They come in both standard and candelabra-size sockets, and adjust from a height of 3¼″ to 4¾″.

A **rigid socket** 2″ high is used in other installations where sockets don't show—many chandelier designs need this type socket, which is also available in both standard and candelabra base.

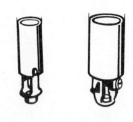

All of these sockets have cardboard insulating sleeves (called paper shells in the trade); each has a regular ⅛-IP female thread at the bottom of the socket that screws onto standard lamp pipe or nipple. These sockets are easy to wire—see page 56 for step-by-step directions.

LAMP SOCKET CLUSTERS

The two most common types of twin-cluster sockets you might have to replace when remodeling old lamps are side-by-side sockets attached to a cluster head (a) and two sockets attached to end of U-shaped arms (b). You can buy either of these clusters with the sockets attached to an adjustable lamp rod (as shown)—some rods adjust in height from 10½″ to 16″.

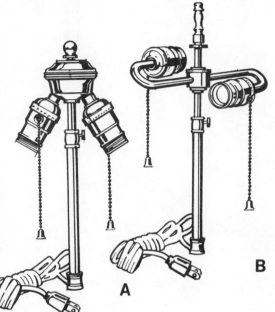

A

B

Or you can buy the cluster head only and keep the original rod. All of these clusters come prewired with 8′ of lamp cord. Simply remove the old cluster head or rod and screw on the new.

FIXTURE SOCKET CLUSTERS

When you need more than one bulb to do a proper lighting job, choose a multiple-fixture socket. It's prewired in two-, three- and four-socket combinations; to install, all you have to deal with are the two lead wires.

Sockets are molded of a phenolic plastic; most common is the twin cluster—two sockets back to back. You can get it keyless, for use with a wall-controlled switch; or with pull chain or turn-knob switch, for swag lights or pull-down fixtures. These sockets are also frequently used for all kinds of installations with bent glass shades and ceiling-hugging fixtures.

The **tandem twin cluster** with sockets side by side, is often used in table-lamp designs. Wire leads on this cluster socket are long enough (24″) to thread through lamp body into base cavity, for splicing to lamp cord.

Tandem cluster has ⅛-IP female threads

187

on each end; the back-to-back clusters have 6″ lead wires and ⅛-IP male threads on each end.

SPACERS

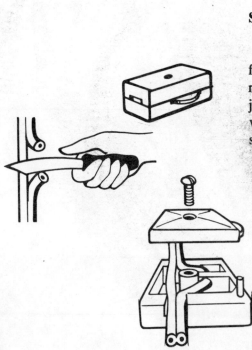

Brass spacers are straight-up-and-down cylinders, which are better for some lamp designs than curved necks (see crackerbox and wheel-hub lamps, Chapter 15). Spacers come ¾″ and ⅞″ in diameter, 2″ or 3″ tall. You need two check rings to seat the spacer, which can then be painted or stained to blend with the lamp.

Plastic spacers simulate candles and are frequently used in electrified candlestick lamps (also called socket covers). They are 1¼″ in diameter and 4″ tall. Or you can buy white plastic candle covers with inside diameters of ¾″ and 1³⁄₁₆″; these covers come precut in ½″ gradations from 2″ to 5″ long; then in 6″, 8″, 12″, 24″, and 36″ tubes—from which you can cut exactly the size you need. Plastic spacers also require seating—you'll need two check rings to finish off the top and bottom.

SWITCHES

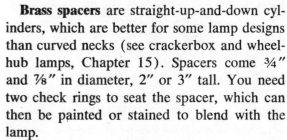

Feed-through cord switch is especially useful when sockets are keyless or in hard-to-reach places. It's small and easy to install—just cut one side of the two parallel lamp-cord wires, lay them in the switch channels, and screw the case shut.

Rotary switch is also used for hard-to-reach or keyless sockets and is often set into the wood or metal base of a table lamp. The two-wire rotary switch lights one or more bulbs—all at the same time. This switch may be controlled by (1) a knob that you turn, (2) button that you push, (3) toggle that you flip; or (4) chain that you pull.

TO INSTALL: Disconnect the lamp; remove the old switch. Loosen small knurled nut of new switch and adjust the hex nut to required height. Slide new switch through opening in lamp base (or fixture) and fasten it firmly with locknut. Connect switch wires to lamp-cord wires with wire nuts.

3-wire rotary switch turns two or more bulbs on alternately. You find it used mostly on table and floor lamps that have candle arms. When wired as shown in the diagram, one twist of the switch will light one bulb, second twist lights two bulbs, third twist all three.

The diagram shows how to wire a floor lamp with three candle arms plus a mogul socket with its own switch:

1. To green switch wire, add one mogul-socket wire and one lamp-stem wire; connect with a wire nut.
2. To red switch wire, add one each of two arm wires; twist together with wire nut.
3. To black switch wire, add one wire from third arm; twist together with wire nut.
4. Combine all other wire ends (five of them —one each from three arms, one from mogul socket, one from stem), and twist together with wire nut.

For a 3-candle table lamp, wire as above, omitting the mogul-socket wires.

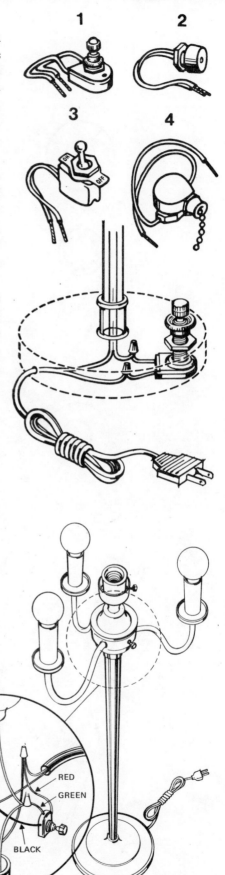

RED
GREEN
BLACK

WASHERS

Steel washers most often used in lamp wiring are small disks with a $\frac{7}{16}''$ center hole that slips over standard lamp pipe. They are usually used with locknuts to relieve friction, distribute pressure, and cover larger-than-$\frac{7}{16}''$ holes. Available in plain or brass-plated steel.

Lockwashers are steel (some are brass-plated) with teeth around the center hole. Like the teeth of a saw, these little prongs are bent alternately to one side and the other, so they bite into surfaces and prevent slipping. Use them between two metal surfaces (between check ring and cap, for instance) to keep them from rotating against each other. Or use between a plain washer and a wood base. As a general guide: wherever a lamp assembly seems loose, add a lockwasher.

Felt or rubber washers are used between metal and glass (or china) surfaces. Even so, don't use force when tightening a nut or screw, lest you crack the glass.

WIRE CONNECTORS

Wire connectors (sometimes called wire nuts) are made of cone-shaped plastic, with a spiral threading on the inside. To use: twist exposed wire ends and insert into cone; turn cone clockwise to lock the wires firmly together. Available in graduated sizes to accommodate from two to five No. 18 wires. They eliminate the need for soldering splices or using insulating tapes.

WIRE STRIPPERS

Wire strippers have notched blades that cut through the insulation covering electric wires —without cutting the wire itself. It's a handy tool to have for exposing wire ends when wiring sockets or installing fixtures.